John

*Not yet published as of this printing.

BIBLE STUDY COMMENTARY

John

HERSCHEL H. HOBBS

Lamplighter Books Grand Rapids, Michigan
Zondervan Publishing House

Printed in the United States of America

90   91   92 / CH / 19   18   17   16

CONTENTS

Introduction

The gospel of John has been called the Holy of Holies of the New Testament. Written in simple language, it rises to the heights and plumbs the depths of spiritual truth. Nowhere else do we find so glorious a picture of Jesus as the Christ of God.

The study of this gospel will prove to be a rich and rewarding experience. Such a study calls for the consideration of certain matters of background material.

The Author and Date. These two items stand together. At one time the date was placed well into the second century, with the suggested author being "the Elder John" of Ephesus or some unknown writer. But discoveries both in the papyri and the Dead Sea Scrolls help to place the date of the gospel's writing in the last quarter of the first century, probably about A.D. 80-90.

This means that the author could be one of the apostles. The gospel itself attributes it to "the disciple whom Jesus loved" (21: 20, 24). Since the Apostle John is not mentioned by name in the gospel, this most likely was his way of referring to himself. There is clear evidence that the author was a Palestinian Jew who was an eyewitness to the events he recorded. It is this author's position that this gospel was written about A.D. 85 by John the apostle "whom Jesus loved."

The Thought Environment. At one time the preponderance of New Testament scholarship, with some exceptions, saw this environment as Greek. But the discovery of the Dead Sea Scrolls has shown it to be primarily Hebrew thought of around A.D. 70. However, the gospel also reflects the fundamental tenets of Gnostic philosophy which existed in Asia Minor during the last quarter of the first century.

Basic in this Gnostic philosophy was the dualistic concept that God was absolutely good and matter was absolutely evil. A good God could not have created the universe. In solving this problem they posited a series of emanations from God in a descending chain. These emanations they called aeons. Each had less of deity than the preceding one. The last aeon possessed enough of deity to create, but not enough to keep from creating evil matter. According to the Gnostics this aeon created the universe, and when they came into contact with Christianity, they identified this lowest aeon with Christ. This would mean that Christ was not God but a demigod, almost a demon.

The Gnostics were divided into two groups in their position on the incarnation of Christ. The Docetics, from the Greek word *dokeō* ("I seem"), said that Christ did not have a flesh and blood body; He only *seemed* to have one. The Cerinthians, from their leader Cerinthus, held that Christ was neither born nor did He die. The aeon Christ came upon Jesus at His baptism, and left Him on the cross. This entire philosophical system cut through the very heart of Christology. John's answer to it appears throughout his gospel, and especially in the Prologue (1:1-18).

Furthermore, from the Hebrew side this gospel contrasts the Mosaic system of law with the Christian revelation of grace. This contrast the author anticipates in John 1:17, and develops in the rest of the gospel. The play upon "light" and "darkness" was once thought to reflect a Grecian influence. But from the Dead Sea Scrolls we have learned that this was a part of Hebrew thought during the last half of the first century. This is a portion of the mysticism found in John's gospel, and which is seen further in the use of such words as "bread," "water," "door," "way," "truth," and "Spirit."

The Purpose of John's Gospel. The author expresses his purpose for us. "But these are written, that ye might believe that Jesus is the Christ, the Son of God; and that believing ye might have life through his name" (20:31).

This purpose is accomplished in a number of ways. The Prologue has such a design. The word "believe" is one of the key words in the book. The Gospel is built about certain "signs" which show forth Jesus' deity. And these, for the most part, were performed in connection with the major feasts of the Jews. These feasts, except for one Passover, furnish the occasions for Jesus' being in Jerusalem, where in connection with some of these "signs" He revealed Himself and His relation to the Father. The "sign" of the raising of Lazarus not only demonstrated Jesus' power over death, but also gave the immediate reason for the Sanhedrin's resolve to put Him to death.

A secondary purpose of the author, and yet a most evident one, was to supplement the synoptic gospels (Matthew, Mark and Luke). The word "synoptic" means a seeing together, describing the gospels which largely present Jesus' ministry from the same point of view; although each, especially Matthew and Luke, contains material all its own.

John's gospel was written after the synoptics. Even when it

parallels them, the author includes significant details not found in the others. The greater body of the gospel deals with a Judean and Jerusalem ministry which is not mentioned in the synoptics. Without this gospel there would be many unanswered questions in the others. For instance, we could not understand fully the Jewish rulers' opposition to Jesus in Galilee. Neither could we completely comprehend why they put Him to death. According to the synoptic gospels, the first time that Jesus went to Jerusalem the Sanhedrin brought Him to the cross. But John supplies the much-needed background information, that Jesus made four previous visits to Jerusalem before the final one. And in each visit John shows us the rising tide of opposition to Jesus which finally erupted during His final visit.

The other gospels fill a definite place in the written revelation of God's full revelation of Himself in Jesus Christ. But John adds meaning to them all. His gospel completes the whole.

HERSCHEL H. HOBBS

First Baptist Church
Oklahoma City, Oklahoma

CHAPTER 1

The Prologue

(John 1:1-18)

Introduction
1. In the Beginning (1:1a)
2. The Eternity of Christ (1:1b)
3. The Equality of Christ (1:1c)
4. The Nature of Christ (1:1d-2)
5. The Creator Christ (1:3)
6. The Christ as Life and Light (1:4, 5)
7. The Witness to the Light (1:6-13, 15)
8. The Word Became Flesh (1:14)
9. Christ, the Fullness of Grace (1:16-18)

John began his gospel in a manner all his own. Mark, writing with the Romans in mind, plunged immediately into the ministry of John the Baptist followed by that of Jesus. The Romans were concerned primarily with what a man did, and not with what he said. Matthew, writing to the Jews, began with Jesus' genealogy (from the standpoint of His foster-father in compliance with legal requirements) which was so important to the Jewish mind. Luke, writing for the Greek mind, first gave his method of research, a matter which would impress his readers. But John, writing long after the others, and in keeping with his mystical nature, began his gospel by presenting Christ in His eternal nature. It was his purpose so to present his Subject that his readers "might believe that Jesus is the Christ, the Son of God" (20:31). Therefore, he took his departure, not from history, but from eternity.

1. *In the Beginning* (1:1a). These words are suggestive of the opening words of Genesis. Whereas Genesis begins with the creation, John goes back behind the creation story into eternity itself, recognizing that God was before creation. But from that

starting point he parallels the creation story in Genesis 1. In fact, a comparison of John 1:1-5 with the opening verses of Genesis 1 shows that John did this by a deliberate design — which shows that while the principal readers of this gospel may have lived in a Greek environment, John's own approach to his task is definitely from the Hebrew standpoint.

The words "in the beginning" are timeless in nature. Even if modern science should prove that the universe is billions of years old, that would not affect these words in either Genesis or John. Whenever the *beginning* was, that is the time of which these Biblical writers are speaking.

2. *The Eternity of Christ* (1:1b). John introduces Christ as eternal. Four times in the first two verses he uses the word "was." This is the imperfect form of the verb "to be" which expresses timeless, essential being. So in effect he says, "In the beginning always was the Word, and the Word always was with God, and the Word always was God. The same always was in the beginning with God."

"In the beginning was the Word." What does John mean by "the Word"? This is the translation of the Greek word *logos* which basically means the spoken word, or an outward revelation from the mind of the one speaking. While John uses this word thirty-six times in the sense of "word" or "saying," he also uses it four times with respect to a person (1:1, 14; note also I John 1:1; Revelation 19:13). In what sense, therefore, does he personify "the Word"?

Various suggestions have been offered. Those who emphasize the Greek influence in and upon this gospel point out classical uses of *logos*. For instance, Heraclitus used it for the principle which maintains order in the universe. The Stoic philosophers used it for the soul of the world. Marcus Aurelius employed it for the generative principle in nature. It is suggested that it may have come into Hebrew thought through Philo, the Jewish-Alexandrian philosopher, who sought to harmonize Greek philosophy with Hebrew theology. Philo used *logos* about thirteen hundred times in his writings, and at times almost personified it, but not quite.

However, those who insist that John is basically Hebrew in thought seek to relate his use of *logos* with "wisdom" in Proverbs 8, where "wisdom" is spoken of as a person. But nowhere does the Old Testament speak of "wisdom" as being eternal. So this source for John's idea is open to question.

Upon what basis, therefore, did John choose the "Word"

to personify Christ? Recalling that John in his first few verses deliberately parallel Genesis 1 throws light upon this question. In the Genesis account of creation each new phase is introduced with the words "And God said." Here, therefore, is the spoken word or outward revelation of God. And this thought is expressed by the Greek word *logos* or Word. It is likely, therefore, that John chose this word to depict God in His outward revelation of Himself. Thus Christ is seen as the person of the Trinity through whom the eternal God reveals Himself both in creation and in redemption. Therefore, "in the beginning always was the Word."

3. *The Equality of Christ* (1:1c). "And the Word was with God." The word "with" translates a Greek word suggesting equality. Literally, "the Word was face to face with God," or the Word saw eye to eye with God, as though they looked at one another on an even line. We are not to think of God as *first* and the Word as *second*, as though the latter was inferior to the former. They are equal, the one to the other.

4. *The Nature of Christ* (1:1d, 2). "And the Word was God." Actually the Greek says "and God was the Word," with "God" in the emphatic position. In English we would say, "And the Word was God Himself." Keeping in mind the meaning of "was," John at the outset makes the stupendous statement that Christ existed eternally on an equality with God, even as God Himself.

This declaration produces a climactic effect at the beginning of the book. Contrary to the Gnostic view that Christ was the lowest aeon in a chain of emanations out of God, whose deity was almost at the vanishing point, John declares that He is God of very God, or God Himself, possesing the sum-total or fullness of deity.

5. *The Creator Christ* (1:3). In verse 3 John declares that Christ is the creator of the universe. Here again he answers the Gnostics. The universe is not a totally evil thing created by an aeon. It is the result of the direct creative activity of Christ who is God Himself.

Note that in this verse John uses a different verb. Whereas in verses 1 and 2 he uses the verb for eternal, essential being, here he uses the verb "to become" or to come into being. The universe, or matter, is not eternal. At a given point in God's timetable it came into being. This is in keeping with the account in Genesis.

In Colossians 1:16 Paul says the same thing. Only he takes the broad sweep as he speaks of Christ as creating the universe as a whole. But even there he mentions the "visible and invisible" (the atom?).

John speaks of the Word creating "all things," meaning each several part of the universe. Thus he says literally, "The universe in its several parts through him came into being; and apart from him came into being not even one thing which has come into being." Christ created the universe from atoms to suns!

6. *The Christ as Life and Light* (1:4, 5). "In him was life; and the life was the light of men." This may just as well read, "In him was light; and the light was the life of men." In this latter sense it parallels the Genesis account. This "life" may mean either the principle of animal life or the principle of spiritual life. And here it probably means both. Furthermore, John is fond of using "light" and "darkness" in their mystical qualities as symbolic of *good* and *evil*. So Christ is the source of all life and light.

At this point John introduces the somber note of the presence of evil in the universe. For "the light keeps on shining in the darkness; and the darkness never was able to overtake it." The picture is that of the darkness chasing the light in an effort to extinguish it. But it was never able to overtake it to accomplish this evil purpose. Once again John alludes to Genesis. "And God called the light Day, and the darkness he called Night. And the evening and the morning were the first day" (Genesis 1:5). In the physical sense evening or darkness chases morning or light, but it is never able to catch up with it. Thus John seizes upon this thought to express the cosmic aspect of the struggle between Christ and Satan, a struggle which he presently presents in the arena of history.

7. *The Witness to the Light* (1:6-13, 15). At this juncture John moves from eternity into time. This he does by introducing John the Baptist, who came into being for the express purpose of bearing testimony to the Light. But having presented him, John the apostle returns to the Light Himself. Christ is the true Light, which lights every man, coming into the world (or the cosmos). Tragic but true, He always was in the world, the world came into being through Him, but the world did not know Him by personal experience.

And this tragedy is compounded by the fact that "He came unto his own, and his own received him not." "His own" is translated from the same words which John uses later to express the idea that the beloved disciple took Mary "unto his own home" (19:27). So, in effect, John says that Christ came "unto his own home," the world which He had created, and those who dwelt upon it did not welcome Him to it. But some did welcome Him. And to those doing so He gave power (right or privilege) to become the sons of God, even to those who believed on His name. These were born not of bloods (plural), or heredity, nor of the will of the flesh (sex), nor of the will of man (willpower), but of God.

8. *The Word Became Flesh* (1:14). The climax of the Prologue is in verse 14. For here John declares that the Word, who always was, who always was equal with God, even God Himself, came into being as flesh. He became what He had never been before. *God became Jesus of Nazareth!*

Once again John strikes a dual blow at the Gnostics. To the Docetics he says that Christ did not merely *seem* to have a flesh and blood body. He *became* flesh. Furthermore, the author adds that he and others beheld His glory. This beholding involved not only the glory at the Transfiguration (cf. Matthew 17), but the entire scope of His dwelling among men. And to the Cerinthian Gnostics John declares that the divinity of Christ did not come upon Jesus at His baptism and leave Him on the cross. Rather, Christ became a flesh and blood man, Jesus of Nazareth.

And "he dwelt among us." The word "dwelt" is akin to the word for "tent" or "tabernacle." It suggests temporary dwelling, or the period of thirty-three years when Jesus was on earth. When viewed as a "tabernacle" the word "glory" adds to the meaning. During Israel's time of worshiping in the Tabernacle, God was said to dwell therein with His people in His Shekinah glory. So for the period of the Incarnation God dwelt with men in His Shekinah glory in a tabernacle of flesh.

Furthermore, He was "full of grace and truth." The word "fullness" was used by the Gnostics to express the sum-total of deity. In their system Christ was said to possess only a small portion of deity. But John declares Him to be "full" of both grace and truth. He was the fullness of God's expression of grace Also, He was the full, complete revelation of God to man. The Greek word for "truth" is formed out of the word, "to conceal," prefixed by the Greek, *alpha* (a), or *alpha privative*, which gives to the basic word the opposite of its meaning. So "truth" means the *unconcealed*. Thus Jesus is the *unconcealed*, or the complete revelation of God.

It is of interest to note that while John does not record the virgin birth of Jesus, he certainly implies it. For Jesus is the "only-born" Son of the Father.

9. *Christ, the Fullness of Grace* (1:16-18). As though to place a spire upon his temple which he has erected to the glory of Christ, John declares, "And of his fulness have all we received, and grace for grace." In Him we have an unlimited supply of

grace. It is grace following after grace. Christ does not give the believer one supply of grace to last him throughout his life. Like manna in the wilderness, He furnishes new grace for each day, each trial, and each task. Out of Him flows an unending stream of grace.

John closes his Prologue by contrasting *law* and *grace*. When God *gave* His law He did so through Moses, a man. But His grace and full revelation *came* in the person of Jesus Christ, who was/is God become man. Moses had longed to see God's face, but could not do so. For no man has ever seen it. But Christ, who is ever in intimate fellowship and equality in the bosom of the Father, has "declared" Him. Literally, He has *exegeted* Him, or has brought forth the full meaning of His person for men to see. Jesus said, "He that hath seen me hath seen the Father" (John 14:9).

And with this John proceeds to recount this unveiling of the Father in His work of redeeming grace. That which had been in the bosom of the Father eternally was wrought out in time.

FOR FURTHER STUDY

1. Read Genesis 1:1-5 and John 1:1-5, noting the parallel ideas in the two passages.
2. Read John 1:1-18 and Colossians 1:12-22 with a view to comparing the similar emphases in these passages of Scripture.
3. Examine the section on Gnostic philosophy in the "Introduction." Then note the ways that John answers these claims regarding creation, the relation of Christ to God and eternity; note especially the author's answer to the Docetic and Cerinthian Gnostics.
4. Read the birth accounts in Matthew 1:18-25 and Luke 1:26-38; 2:1-12, and then study John 1:14 in this light.
5. Read the article on "Logos" in Hastings *Dictionary of the Bible* (Scribners), pp. 549-51, or in some other Bible Dictionary. Note the use of "Logos" in I John 1:1; 5:7; and Revelation 19:13.
6. List some physical characteristics of "light" and "darkness," and relate them to spiritual truth.
7. What are some of the ways in which darkness seeks to extinguish the Light?

CHAPTER 2

The Time Of Beginning

(THE FIRST PASSOVER)
(John 1:19 - 4:54)

Introduction
1. The Witness of John the Baptist (1:19-34)
2. The First Disciples of Jesus (1:35-51)
3. The Beginning of "Signs" (2:1-11)
4. The Cleansing of the Temple (2:12-25)
5. The Interview With Nicodemus (3:1-21)
6. The Relationship Between Jesus and John the Baptist (3:22-36)
7. The Interview With the Woman in Samaria (4:1-42)
8. Jesus in Galilee (4:43-54)

The first year of Jesus' public ministry has been called a year of obscurity. It was a year of preparation before He entered into His Galilean ministry, a ministry which is recorded largely in the other three gospels. In keeping with his purpose to supplement their accounts, John, with the exception of one event, chose to by-pass this period. However, he takes note of the fact that Jesus did spend a great deal of time in Galilee and its environs. But apart from the events surrounding the baptism of Jesus and His wilderness temptation, we are largely indebted to John for the record of this first year in our Lord's ministry.

1. *The Witness of John the Baptist* (1:19-34). When John the Baptist came preaching in the wilderness of Judea great crowds swarmed to hear him. The Jewish rulers in Jerusalem even sent a delegation to investigate matters. To them the Baptist emphatically denied that he was the Christ. He was only "the voice of one crying in the wilderness" (v. 23; Isaiah 40:3). He was the forerunner of the Christ.

Finally, when the Baptist had baptized Jesus he was given

17

from heaven a previously arranged sign by which he would recognize the Christ (vv. 32, 33). Seeing the Spirit of God as a dove descend upon Jesus, he bore witness that He was the Son of God. Furthermore, he had declared Him to be "the Lamb of God, which taketh away the sin of the world" (v. 29).

2. *The First Disciples of Jesus* (1:35-51). On one occasion the Baptist pointed two of his disciples to Jesus, saying, "Behold the Lamb of God" (v. 36). Thereafter, they left him to follow Jesus (vv. 37-40). One of these was Andrew, the brother of Simon Peter. The other is anonymous, but probaly was John, the author of this gospel. More than half a century later he remembered the exact time of day when he began to follow Jesus, ten o'clock in the morning (v. 39).

As soon as these disciples left Jesus, Andrew sought out his brother Simon, declaring that they had found the Christ (v. 41). He brought Simon to Jesus, who prophesied the day when he would be called *Cephas,* a stone, which is the Aramaic equivalent of the Greek word rendered *Peter.*

The following day Jesus began His journey back to Galilee, for His home was in Nazareth. On the way He met Philip and said to him, "Follow me" (v. 43). Philip then found Nathanael who, after some hesitation, came to Jesus also (vv. 45, 46). And Nathanael became so completely convinced concerning Jesus that he said, "Rabbi, thou art the Son of God; thou art the King of Israel" (v. 49).

So Jesus had made a beginning. He had called His first disciples. And their number would continue to grow as others believed "that Jesus is the Christ, the Son of God; and that believing [they] might have life through his name" (20:31).

3. *The Beginning of "Signs"* (2:1-11). One significant feature of John's gospel is his use of the word "sign" to refer to the miracles of Jesus. These miracles were signs of His deity. John largely builds his account of Jesus' ministry about these signs. And the first of them he records in chapter 2.

Upon His return to Galilee Jesus, along with His mother and disciples, was a guest at a marriage feast in Cana. He was a social being, quite unlike the stern asceticism of John the Baptist.

During the feast the wine ran out. Mary brought the problem to Jesus. But He said, "Woman, what have I to do with thee? mine hour has not yet come" (v. 4). Literally, "What to me and to you?" As guests this matter was not their concern.

Some see in the term, "woman," a note of disrespect. But the Greek word rendered thereby connotes both respect and affection.

At the same time it expresses the idea of a respectful distance. When it is coupled with Jesus' statement that His hour had not yet come, it suggests that He was saying gently that in His present relationship He should no longer be regarded by her in the sense of mother and son. He is both her Lord and her Saviour. Their relationship is no longer merely genetical but spiritual. Even though Jesus most likely called her "mother" in the home in Nazareth, it is significant that nowhere in the gospels does He use that word in direct address to her. He uses the word "woman."

The reference to Jesus' "hour" is the first of several that He used to refer to the cross. But in this particular context it could mean the full manifestation of Himself as the Christ of God. This complete unveiling of God's love would be His death on the cross.

Nevertheless, Jesus miraculously met the social emergency by turning water into wine, a wine which the ruler of the feast declared to be better than that which had been served first (v. 10). Knowing the mystical nature of John, one cannot help but see the inferred lesson. The "wine," or way of life, which Jesus provides, is better than that which was available under the Law or under the Jewish system of religion.

But John clearly states his primary purpose in recording this "sign." It was the first of many which revealed the glory of Christ. And the disciples, who already believed in Him, had their faith strengthened thereby (v. 11).

4. *The Cleansing of the Temple* (2:12-25). After a brief visit to Capernaum, a city located on the northwest shore of the Sea of Galilee (which later would become Jesus' Galilean headquarters), He made a visit to Jerusalem. This was the first of several such visits during His public ministry, and which are recorded only by John (except the final one). The occasion for this initial visit was the Passover, the greatest feast among the Jews. It commemorated Israel's deliverance from Egyptian bondage, a central feature of which was the slaying of the paschal lamb.

When Jesus arrived in Jerusalem, He entered the temple area. There, in the Court of the Gentiles, instead of an atmosphere of worship, He found it as noisy and confused as an Oriental bazaar. In fact, He found what was commonly called "The Bazaars of Annas." Annas was a former high priest who had been deposed by the Romans. Several of his sons had followed him in the office. The present high priest, Caiaphas, was his son-in-law.

What had begun as a service to the worshipers had now become a racket. Those who came to the Passover did so to make

certain sacrifices. It was often difficult for them to bring along
their oxen, sheep, or doves for this purpose. This was especially
true of those from outside Palestine. So provision was made for
their purchase at the temple. Furthermore, at this season every
male adult Jew was required to pay the half shekel temple tax
— in that Jewish coin. It might be paid in one's village. Otherwise
it must be paid at the temple. Usually those pilgrims from outside Palestine paid it there. And Roman or other coins had to be
exchanged for the Jewish coin.

These *services* had become a means of exploitation. Exhor-
bitant prices were charged. The profits were supposed to go into
the temple treasury. But much of them found their way into the
pockets of those who rendered the service.

Not only was it an unscrupulous business, but it was an of-
fense to Gentiles who might enter this court to worship. So in
righteous indignation Jesus drove from the temple both the mer-
chants and their animals. He poured out the changers' money and
overturned their tables. To the sellers of doves He said, "Take
these things hence; make not my Father's house a house of mer-
chandise" or an emporium (v. 16).

Quite naturally the Jewish rulers were indignant. Their source
of ill-gotten gain was destroyed. Furthermore, according to them,
such authority over the temple was supposed to be exercised only
by a prophet or by the Messiah. So they challenged Jesus' authority.
"What sign shewest thou unto us, seeing that thou doest these
things?" (v. 18).

Jesus replied, "Destroy this temple, and in three days I will
raise it up again" (v. 19). Herod's temple had been begun in
20-19 B.C. It was not finished until A.D. 64, just six years
prior to its destruction by the Roman Titus. So at the time when
Jesus spoke it had been under construction for forty-six years.
Did Jesus propose to rebuild it in three days? Later the Jewish
rulers used this claim as a charge against Him at His trial.

John, writing long after Jesus' Resurrection, notes that He spoke
of the temple of His body. So even at this early stage in His
ministry Jesus prophesied His bodily Resurrection (vv. 21, 22).

Thus ended Jesus' first clash with the Jewish rulers and their
empty religious system of formalism and of the oppression of the
people. But it was not to be the last. In the end these rulers truly
would "destroy this temple." But God would raise it up on the
third day.

Although the Jewish rulers refused to believe on Jesus, there
were many at the feast who did — because of the signs which He

did. Even so, He did not fully commit Himself to them, for He knew the fickle nature of men (vv. 23-25).

5. *The Interview With Nicodemus* (3:1-21). One such *believer* was Nicodemus, a Pharisee and a member of the Sanhedrin, the ruling body among the Jews. He sought out Jesus. But he did so by night, probably to avoid publicity and to guarantee an uninterrupted interview (vv. 1, 2). He greeted Jesus with the words, "Rabbi, we know that thou art a teacher come from God: for no man can do these miracles [signs] that thou doest, except God be with him" (v. 2). This teacher of Israel recognized this unaccredited rabbi from Nazareth as being accredited by God.

In reply to Nicodemus Jesus came directly to the point. "Except a man be born again [or from above], he cannot see the kingdom of God" (v. 3). Simply being born a Jew did not entitle one to kingdom citizenship. This was quite a shock to Nicodemus. Did Jesus mean that he must experience a second physical birth? But Jesus pressed His point. "Except a man be born of water and of the Spirit, he cannot enter into the kingdom of God" (v. 5).

What did Jesus mean by being "born of water and of the Spirit"? Some interpret "born of water" to refer to *baptismal regeneration,* contrary to the overall teaching of the New Testament. Others see the combination of *water* and *spirit* as representing one act, the *cleansing of regeneration.* In view of John's mysticism this is a possible meaning. Another group sees "born of water" as referring to the *physical birth* in contrast to "born of the Spirit" or *spiritual birth.* But whatever the meaning, it is clear that the discussion centered in the contrast of the physical and spiritual births (v. 6). By the former birth, one is born into natural relationships. By the latter birth, one is born into spiritual relationships. Therefore, "ye must be born again" (v. 7).

In an effort to clear up the mystery for Nicodemus Jesus compared "wind" (*pneuma*) with "spirit" (*pneuma*) (vv. 8-13). Failing here He resorted to Scripture, a subject with which Nicodemus was familiar (vv. 14, 15). He referred to the incident of the brazen serpent in the wilderness. Moses lifted it up so that all who believed God's promise would be healed from serpent bites. 'Even so must the Son of man be lifted up [on the cross]: that whosoever believeth in him should not perish, but have eternal life." The key word is "believeth." So Nicodemus will not be born again through understanding, but by faith in God's promise through His Son.

Scholars are divided as to whether John 3:16-21 are Jesus'

words or John's comment upon what Jesus had said. There is no valid reason for not regarding them as Jesus' own words.

One can only speak of John 3:16 in superlatives. It tells of the greatest cause for love (for), the greatest lover (God), the greatest degree of love (so loved), the greatest object of love (the world), the greatest demonstration of love (that), the greatest expression of love (he gave), the greatest gift of love (his only begotten Son), the greatest provision of love (that), the greatest recipients of love (whosoever), the greatest response to love (believeth on him), the greatest deliverance of love (should not perish), the greatest alternative of love (but), and the greatest result of love (have everlasting life). It is impossible to pour more gospel truth into one verse than this which is called "the little Gospel."

Furthermore, Jesus added that His mission was not one of judgment but of salvation to all who would believe in Him (vv. 17-21). Whether or not Nicodemus received Him as his Saviour at this time is not stated. But the gospel seed had been sown, and in time it did yield an abundant harvest in his life.

6. *The Relationship Between Jesus and John the Baptist* (3:22-36). Following His visit to Jerusalem, Jesus spent some time in Judea. Many people, believing on Him, were baptized by His disciples. This growing popularity caused disciples of the Baptist to point out the fact to him. But he made it clear to them that this was as it should be. He was but the friend of the Bridegroom who had made arrangements for the wedding. Now that the Bridegroom has appeared, he rejoices as he recedes into the background. And it will continue to be so. For "he must go on increasing, but I must go on decreasing" (v. 30).

The remainder of chapter 3 is the author's comments on the Baptist. The Baptist had done his work well. Now the earthly messenger steps from the stage in order that the spotlight may focus on Him "that cometh from heaven." And "he that believeth on the Son hath everlasting life: and he that believeth not the Son shall not see life; but the wrath of God abideth on him" (v. 36).

7. *The Interview With the Woman in Samaria* (4:1-42). Because of the Pharisees' jealousy over Jesus' growing popularity, He left Judea to return to Galilee. The synoptic gospels give an additional reason, the arrest of John the Baptist by Herod Antipas, the tetrarch of Galilee and Perea. Herod must have been at Machaerus, a fortress east of the Dead Sea, where the Baptist was imprisoned. So Jesus left the vicinity to get as far from the wily ruler as possible and still remain in his territory.

John notes that Jesus "must needs go through Samaria" (v. 4). This was the normal route to take from Judea to Galilee. When Jews traveled southward they usually avoided the country of the Samaritans by going through Perea, an area east of the Jordan. This was because the Samaritans might abuse anyone passing through their land and journeying to Judea.

The hatred between the Jews and Samaritans probably dated from the conflicts between the kingdoms of Judah and Israel. It was enhanced following the fall of the northern kingdom (722 B.C.), when the Israelites who were left in the land intermarried with imported foreigners to produce the Samaritan people. The opposition of the Samaritans to the rebuilding of the walls of Jerusalem after the Babylonian captivity added further to this hostile relationship.

However, John's note as to the necessity of Jesus going through Samaria carries not so much a geographical as a spiritual meaning. The necessity lay in the experience which awaited Him there.

About six o'clock in the evening Jesus arrived at Jacob's well near Sychar, a village located about forty-two miles north of Jerusalem. The disciples had gone into the village to buy food. Jesus was left alone as He rested at the well. Then a woman of shady character came out of the village to get water. Jesus' body was thirsty, but His soul thirsted for her soul the more. Therefore, He began a conversation with her as He asked, "Give me to drink" (v. 7).

This simple question began one of the classic soul-winning efforts of all time. In Jerusalem Jesus had dealt with Nicodemus, an honored man in Jewish society. Now He was dealing with a woman of shame in Samaritan society. And as He did so He led her from scorn, to curiosity, to interest, to respect, and finally to faith.

The woman met Jesus' simple request with a question. "How is it that thou, being a Jew, askest drink of me, which am a woman of Samaria? for the Jews have no dealings with the Samaritans" (v. 9). We may be sure that she pronounced the word "Jew" with *scorn*. Her answer contained the prejudices of race, religion, and sex. But Jesus brushed them all aside as He offered her living water (v. 10). This aroused her *curiosity*. How could He give her this water, since He had nothing with which to draw it from the well (vv. 11, 12)? She was thinking of natural water. Jesus struck a note of *interest* when He told her that if she drank the water that He gave she would never thirst again (vv. 13, 14). Remembering the long walk from Sychar she said, "Sir, give me this water, that I thirst not, neither come hither to draw" (v. 15). She still did not realize her spiritual need.

So He probed more deeply as He revealed His knowledge of her sinful life (vv. 16-18). This show of knowledge by Jesus generated her *respect* (vv. 19-26). "Sir, I perceive that thou art a prophet" (v. 19). But to avoid this embarrasing subject she resorted to the religious controversy as to the true place of worship, Mt. Gerizim or Jerusalem. Jesus circumvented the controversy by teaching her the true nature of God and of worship. She did not argue the point further. Instead, she adopted a delaying tactic by pointing out that when the Messiah comes "he will tell us all things" (v. 25). Jesus brought the matter to a head by saying, "I that speak unto thee am he" (v. 26).

With this she became a woman of *faith*. She ran to the village to tell others about Him. "Come, see a man, which told me all things that ever I did: is not this the Christ?" (v. 29). She put her expression of faith in the form of a question simply to avoid the criticism of the men.

In the meantime the disciples had returned to Jesus and wondered that He was talking to this woman (v. 27). He replied by pointing out to them the rich harvest of souls which was waiting to be gathered (vv. 31-38).

A token of this harvest was seen in the group which arrived at the well from Sychar (vv. 39-42). At their request Jesus remained in their village for two days. Sychar experienced a great revival as seen in the people's statement to the woman. "Now we believe, not because of thy saying: for we have heard him ourselves, and know that this is indeed the Christ, the Saviour of the world" (v. 42). Not of the Jews or Samaritans only, but "of the world."

8. *Jesus in Galilee* (4:43-54). Back in Galilee Jesus healed the son of a nobleman, probably one of the officers of Herod Antipas. The significant thing about this is that the son was in Capernaum and Jesus was in Cana, some miles away. So Jesus healed by a word and from a distance. When the father was going home, believing Jesus' word, his servants met him along the way. And he learned that his son's fever had left him at the very time when Jesus had said, "Go thy way; thy son liveth" (vv. 50, 52, 53).

In closing chapter 4, John notes that this was the second "sign" which Jesus had wrought in Galilee. It is also worthy of note that this is the only event recorded by John which is a part of Jesus' great Galilean ministry. This portion, which covered about eighteen months, had been recorded by the synoptic gospels. So, true to his purpose, John touched upon it, and then proceeded to major on hitherto unrecorded events of Jesus' ministry in Jerusalem and Judea.

FOR FURTHER STUDY

1. Read the fuller accounts of John the Baptist's ministry in Matthew 3:1-17; Mark 1:1-11; Luke 3:1-18, 21-23.
2. Compare John 1:45-51 with Genesis 28:10-19. Was Nathanael dreaming of the "good old days"? Do Jesus' words to him show Jesus' knowledge of his thoughts? Was this the thing which brought forth Nathanael's declaration of faith?
3. Locate Cana on a map of Palestine in the time of Christ. Note its proximity to both Nazareth and Capernaum. A study of this map will help the student better to understand the gospel of John.
4. Read the article on "Passover . . ." in Hastings *Dictionary of the Bible*, or in *Zondervan's Pictorial Bible Dictionary*.
5. In the same volumes read the article on Herod's temple.
6. Read the second cleansing of the temple (Mark 11:15-18). Note that Jesus cleansed the temple at the beginning and end of His public ministry.
7. To understand more clearly the imprisonment and fate of John the Baptist, read Mark 6:14-29.

CHAPTER 3

The Second Visit To Jerusalem

(THE SECOND PASSOVER)
(John 5)

Several months of the Galilean ministry had elapsed between John 4 and 5. Jesus had called five of His disciples (Peter, Andrew, James, John and Matthew) to leave their means of livelihood to follow Him in His work. With the first four He had made a preaching tour of Galilee. These things we learn from the synoptic gospels.

1. *After This* (5:1a). Now in chapter 5 John says that "after this" Jesus made a return visit to Jerusalem. "After this" should read "after these things." John does not mean that this visit occured immediately after the healing of the nobleman's son (4:46-54). Or else we might wonder why Jesus would go to Galilee only to return immediately to Jerusalem. The time element between 4:54 and 5:1 is expressed in this phrase "after these things." It is a phrase found repeatedly in John (cf. 6:1; 7:1; 19:38; 21:1) to indicate that he is adding a body of material not found in the synoptic gospels. He assumes their record, and then proceeds to supplement it.

2. *A Feast of the Jews* (5:1b). To what feast does this refer? Several have been suggested (Purim, Passover, Pentecost, Tabernacles, Dedication). The context seems to favor one of the first two. Since Purim was a minor feast, it is unlikely that Jesus would have gone to Jerusalem for it. He would have done so for the Passover. The identity of this feast is important in determining the length of Jesus' ministry. If this were not a Passover, it would mean a ministry of about two and one-half years. But if it was a Passover, this would indicate clearly a ministry of three and one-half years. In all likelihood the latter is the case.

3. *Jesus Went Up to Jerusalem* (5:1c). This statement points to the author as being one who was familiar with the topography of Palestine. To go from Galilee to Jerusalem would be to go south or *down*. But one who thought topographically would say "up," since Jerusalem was located in the mountains. From any direction, except from Hebron to the south, one went *up* to Jerusalem.

This simple fact has a direct bearing on the authorship of this gospel. Evidently he was a Palestinian Jew, and most likely John the beloved disciple.

4. *The Pool of Bethesda* (5:2, 3). Again the author shows a knowledge of Jerusalem prior to its destruction in A.D. 70. For he locates this pool by the "sheep gate" (RV); literally, "the pertaining to a sheep." This probably refers to the "sheep gate" mentioned in Nehemiah (3:1, 32; 12:39), which was located at the eastern extremity of the north wall of the city.

Near this gate was a large pool called Bethesda, meaning "the house of mercy." John says that it had five porches, a covered colonnade built about the pool. The pool was formed by a spring which flowed intermittently, causing the water to be troubled. Jewish belief had it that an angel disturbed the pool, and that the first sick person to get into the water thereafter was healed. (But note that John 5:4 does not appear in the best manuscripts. It was probably added later to explain verses 3 and 5ff.). At any rate this Jewish belief explains the presence of the many sick people about the pool.

Through the years various pools have been suggested as possibly being the pool of Bethesda. But none of them concurs with John's location of it. In 1888 a pool was discovered in the area mentioned by him. It was found that the Crusaders had built a church over it. In recent years excavation of this site has been in progress. It conforms to John's description, porches and all. In all probability this is the pool of Bethesda.

5. *The Healing of a Lame Man* (5:5-9a). John says that

among those about the pool was a man "which had an infirmity thirty and eight years" (v. 5). Evidently he was crippled in his legs. When Jesus saw him He asked if he wished to be healed. He did. But he pointed out that after the water was troubled, someone else always beat him into the pool. Imagine his surprise when Jesus said, "Rise, take up thy bed [pallet], and walk" (v. 8). But he did as he was commanded. "Immediately the man was made whole." The verb tense and the word "immediately" both testify that this was a miracle, or another "sign."

6. *The Sabbath Controversy* (5:9b-13). With dramatic effect John sounds an ominous note. "And on the same day was the sabbath" (v. 9b). Thus John introduces the conflict between the Jewish rulers and Jesus regarding healing on the Sabbath day. From the synoptic gospels we know that Jesus had already healed on the Sabbath (Mark 1:21-34; Luke 4:31-40). But this healing had occurred in Jerusalem, the seat of Jewish power. And the controversy which began here continued throughout Jesus' ministry.

To understand this we must note the place of the Sabbath in the Jewish religious system. Four things occupied a central place in it: the temple, the law, traditions, and the Sabbath. But of all these only the Sabbath was unique in the Jewish religion. Other religions had their temples, scriptures, and traditions. But Judaism alone had the Sabbath. Therefore, the Jews were unusually sensitive at this point. Much of the conflict between Jesus and the Jews centered in these four items. He had already claimed authority over the temple. Later He will do the same with regard to the law (Matthew 5:21ff.). He will reject the Jewish traditions (Matthew 15:1-20; Mark 7:1-23) and He will also declare His Lordship over the Sabbath (Matthew 12:8; Mark 2:28; Luke 6:5). This He will do on His way back to Galilee following this visit to Jerusalem (cf. Mark 2:23-28). Therefore, John's note that the healing of the crippled man occurred on the Sabbath marks the beginning of this continuing controversy, because Jesus dared to challenge the Jews at the point of the unique institution in their religion.

A further word should be said with respect to the observance of the Sabbath. The fourth commandment simply said that men should keep the Sabbath day holy, and that they should refrain from labor on that day. But the Jews had devised hundreds of regulations tending toward defining what constituted *work*. For instance, they permitted only a Sabbath day's journey which was 3,600 feet, or a little less than three-fourths of a mile. A person could not pull a head of grain from the stalk on the Sabbath, for that was reaping. Or rub out the grains in the palms of his hands, for that was threshing. One was forbidden to carry any kind of burden on the Sabbath. Learned (?) debates were held over whether one could treat a sore throat on the Sabbath. It was finally concluded that he might drink oil for food. If it helped his throat, that was incidental.

In this light, therefore, it is understandable that the Jews were shocked to see the healed man carrying his pallet on the Sabbath day. Apparently they did not yet know of the miracle. If they recognized the man as the former cripple, that would make their attitude all the more despicable. Nevertheless, they said nothing about healing. They merely challenged the man for bearing a burden on that day. And to note how serious a crime this was to them, rabbinical law prescribed stoning to death for such a violation.

The man told them that the one who had made him whole told him to take up his bed, and walk. When the Jews asked the man's identity, he could not tell them. In his excitement he had not even learned the name of his benefactor. And, besides, Jesus had slipped away in the crowd.

7. *The Benefactor Identified* (5:14-18). Later Jesus found the man in the temple area. Perhaps he had gone there to give thanks for his healing. Or he may have been simply wandering about. For the word "findeth" implies that Jesus conducted a search. He had a greater blessing in store for the man than just healing his body. "Behold, thou art made whole: sin no more, lest a worse thing befall thee" (5:14). This does not necessarily mean that the man's crippled condition had been due to some specific sin, although it could have been. We may understand Jesus' words to mean that there is a worse thing than being crippled, even for thirty-eight years. That would be the eternal loss of one's soul. The man's restored condition might even be an encourgement to sin. And such sin now would surely be one of knowledge, since he had come face to face with Jesus.

Apparently, this time the man asked Jesus His name. For he went "and told the Jews that it was Jesus, which had made him whole" (v. 15). This act could be interpreted in one of two ways. Either he did so, regardless of what it might do to Jesus, in order to clear himself with the Jews, lest he be stoned. Or else he did so without realizing what the consequences could mean to his Benefactor.

But regardless of the motive, his information brought the wrath of the Jewish rulers down upon Jesus. For because He healed on the Sabbath, they began to persecute Him. The word "persecute" (v. 16) means that they began to persecute Him and continued to do so. They did this not because He had healed the man, but because He did so on the Sabbath day. They were more concerned about the day than about the man. However, some of them will soon hear Jesus say, "The sabbath was made for man, and not man for the sabbath: therefore the Son of man is Lord also of the sabbath" (Mark 2:27, 28).

The Jewish rulers had long been opposed to Jesus. They resented His act in cleansing the temple. They feared His growing popularity, which they saw as a threat to their own position. Now they had an issue, Jesus' conduct on the Sabbath. And they will play it to the hilt. It should be noted, however, that Jesus never violated the divine intent of the Sabbath day. He simply ignored the rote rules of the Pharisees, and sought to restore the day to its proper place. It was to be a blessing and not a burden to men.

Jesus' answer to His critics was, "My Father worketh hitherto, and I work" (v. 17). Actually, He said that His Father "keeps on working," even on the Sabbath, "and I keep on working." This He had done as He healed the crippled man. Note that He did not say "our Father," but "My Father." Thus He claimed a unique relationship with the Father. Furthermore, in His words, "And I," He claimed equality with the Father. The Jews caught this point. Therefore, all the more they kept seeking to kill Him. To them He not only was a habitual Sabbath-breaker, He also called God "his own Father" (v. 18, literal translation), thus making Himself equal with God. Their *continued seeking* to kill Jesus spans the remainder of His earthly ministry.

8. *The Son and the Father* (5:19-30). But despite their threats Jesus did not retreat from His claim with relation to the Father. Instead, He pressed it all the more. He said that the Son can do nothing of Himself, "but what he seeth the Father do." Or, literally, "unless he sees the Father doing it." He sees the Father working, and He works likewise. The Father works benevolently on the Sabbath, and the Son does likewise. He was doing this very thing when He healed the impotent man.

Because of the intimate love between the Father and the Son, the latter perfectly understands the work of the former. And there are greater works to come. If they marvel at Jesus healing a crippled man, they will have occasion to marvel more. Because as the Father gives life to the dead, even so the Son will do as He wills. The synoptic gospels record that Jesus raised from the dead the widow's son at Nain and the daughter of Jairus. But John himself records that Jesus raised Lazarus from the dead.

Furthermore, the Father has committed all judgment to the Son. Actually, He "has given" it, which means that it is a permanent commitment. "For the Father [Himself] judges no man" (v. 22). For this reason, "all men should honour the Son, even as they honour the Father" (v. 23). In these words Jesus claimed the right to be worshiped along with the Father. And, in essence, He added that those who do not worship Him do not truly worship God.

Because all judgment has been given to Him, men should take heed as to how they relate themselves to Him. Therefore, Jesus said, "He that heareth my word, and believeth on him that sent me, hath everlasting life, and shall not come into condemnation [judgment]; but is passed from death unto life" (v. 24). Those who through faith in the Father receive Him whom the Father has sent will have everlasting life. They will not come to judgment, for they already will have been judged in Christ. There will be no second death for them, because already they will have been passed from death unto life.

Notice the assurance which Jesus gives in this verse. Every verb in it, except one, is a present tense. "Shall not come" is a present tense with a future effect. The other verb, "is passed," is a perfect tense in the Greek, expressing a finished or completed work with no possibility of being changed.

Jesus continues this thought of a present salvation when He says, "The hour is coming, *and now is,* when the dead shall hear the voice of the Son of God: and they that hear shall live" (v. 25, author's italics). He is speaking of the spiritually dead hearing and heeding His voice. And those who do so shall live spiritually. This is because the Son has life within Himself, even as the Father has life within Himself. "In him was life; and the life was the light of men" (1:4).

Now Jesus looks beyond the present to the final judgment, the authority for which the Father has given Him. Because of this authority the hour is coming when all who are in their graves will rise at His voice. The saved will come forth "unto the resurrection of life." The lost shall do likewise, but "unto the resurrection of damnation" or judgment (v. 29). Note again that the saved will have been judged already in Christ.

But, even so, this judgment will not be the Son's alone. He will judge according to the Father's will, a will that He knows perfectly. Therefore, in truth, His judgment will be a righteous judgment, and one from which there is no appeal.

9. *The Witness to the Son* (5:31-47). Here Jesus anticipates
the Jews' objection that He cannot alone bear witness of Himself.
It must be substantiated by that of others. In Jewish, Greek, and
Roman law the witness of one is not received in his own case.
So Jesus proceeds to call the roll of those who witness concern-
ing Him.

First, there was John the Baptist (v. 33). He bore witness
to the truth. But Jesus adds that He does not rely upon this witness to corroborate His claims. For his authority was not of human
origin. However, He cites him for the sake of His audience, because they were familiar with the preaching of the Baptist. He
was a burning and shining light. They had heard him, and for
a season were thrilled by him. But they soon lost interest in him
when he disclaimed any Messianic role.

Second, there was the witness of Jesus' works (v. 36). The
disciples had seen His "sign" in Cana, and had believed in Him.
He had shown other such "signs," including the healing of the
crippled man. However, the Jewish rulers ignored them. But their
ignoring them did not discount them as evidence that Jesus had
been sent by the Father.

Third, there was the witness of the Father Himself (v. 37).
This could refer back to the "voice" at Jesus' baptism. But even
His works were evidence that a supernatural power worked in
Him. Nicodemus had recognized Him as one sent from God because of His "signs." But these present critics had seen such, yet
had not believed in Him. To Jesus this was evidence that they had
not heard the Father's voice, had not seen Him, and His word did
not abide in them.

Fourth, there was the witness of the Scriptures (v. 39).
Literally, Jesus said, "Ye search the scriptures; for in them ye think
ye have eternal life: and they are they which testify of me. And
ye will not come unto me, that ye might have life" (vv. 39, 40).

The Jews were ardent students of the Old Testament Scriptures. And they thought that a careful study of the Old Testament
would give them eternal life. Here Jesus does not condemn them
for their study, but for the method and purpose which they used.
They so studied the *letter* that they missed the *spirit.* Had they
searched the Scriptures with spiritual discernment, they would have
known that He was their fulfillment. Jesus Himself unfolded this fact
to His disciples (Luke 24:27, 44-46). But blinded by the me-
chanics, the Jews missed the dynamic. And in rejecting Jesus,
they rejected life.

The tragedy is that while the Jews did not receive Christ, they

were constantly being deluded by false messiahs (v. 43). They
honored one another, but refused to honor Him who was sent
from God. Therefore, they could expect only judgment from
Him whom they claimed to judge.

Fifth, there was the witness of Moses (v. 45). This was the
climax of Jesus' argument. For the Jews claimed to follow Moses'
teachings to the letter. They had set their hope of glory on this.
But Jesus accuses them of not even believing Moses. For "he
wrote of me" (v. 46, cf. Deuteronomy 18:18f.). Had they believed
Moses, they would have believed Him. But since they did not
believe even Moses' writings, how could they expect to believe
the words of Jesus (v. 47)?

John does not record any reply which the Jews made to Jesus.
Indeed, there probably was none. His panel of witnessess was
overwhelming. Jesus had established His case, even though the
Jews refused to accept the fact. In their minds they were unable
to answer Him. This served not to convince them, but merely to
wound their intellectual pride. And this hardened their hearts all
the more.

Jesus, therefore, departed from Jerusalem to return to Galilee.
John is silent about the year of intensive activity which followed
in Galilee. This was fully recorded in the synoptic gospels. Therefore, in keeping with his purpose, he by-passes this period to pick
up the story again "after these things" (6:1).

FOR FURTHER STUDY

1. For a discussion of the "feast" in John 5:1 read A. T. Robertson's *A Harmony of the Gospels*, pp. 267-270.
2. Examine a map of Palestine to understand better the topography of the area. Cf. John 5:1c, "up."
3. For a brief article on the pool of Bethesda read Vardaman's
   Archaeology and the Living Word (Broadman), pp. 102-104.
4. Matthew 12:1-14; Mark 2:23 - 3:6; Luke 6:1-11 record events
   coming immediately after John 5. Read these passages to see
   how the Sabbath controversy begun in John 5 continued on
   Jesus' return to Galilee.
5. In John 5 Jesus began clearly to show His identity with the
   Father. Read carefully John 5:17-47, noting certain points
   of this identity.

CHAPTER 4

The Climax Of The Galilean Ministry

(THE THIRD PASSOVER)
(John 6)

John introduces this chapter with his phrase, "after these things" (v. 1). In this instance the phrase covered one entire year and involved the heart of Jesus' Galilean ministry. At its close He began a series of withdrawals from Galilee, involving a period of about six months from the Passover to the feast of Tabernacles (A.D. 29).

The first of these withdrawals was to an area east of the Sea of Galilee. It is at this point that John joins the account of the synoptic gospels in recounting the feeding of the five thousand. Only here does he parallel them prior to the last week in Jerusalem. His purpose in doing so here is to set the background for Jesus' teachings on the following day, and to mark the climax of His Galilean ministry.

1. *A Miraculous Feeding* (6:2-13). When Jesus arrived on the eastern shore of the Sea of Galilee, He found that a multitude of people from Galilee had preceded Him there. John notes the time as being just prior to the Passover (v. 4). It was about the middle of the afternoon. Knowing that the people were hungry, Jesus asked Philip where they might buy food with which to feed them. Yet John notes that He knew all the while what He would do. Philip protested that two hundred denarii (about $34.00) worth of bread would not feed this group. Andrew suggested that a lad had five barley loaves (cakes) and two small fishes, the food of the poor. "But what are they among so many?" he asked (v. 9). Neither Philip nor Andrew reckoned with the power of Jesus.

Jesus told them to have the people to sit down in groups of hundreds and fifties (synoptics). Note Jesus' use of organization. John calls attention to the fact that there was much grass there (v. 10). He was an eyewitness to the event. Mark further makes the picture vivid, perhaps through the eyes of Peter said by tradition to be the source of Mark's material. Mark describes the groups as "garden beds" (6:40). Their colorful garments looked like flower beds nestled among the green grass.

Then Jesus, after thanks, began to break the bread and fish. In turn His disciples distributed the food among the people. The more Jesus broke, the more He had. It was more than enough to feed the crowd. For afterward they gathered up twelve baskets full, not of scraps, but of uneaten food. Jesus wasted nothing that He had made.

Various attempts have been made to explain away this miracle or "sign." It has been suggested that the disciples found a cache of food in a cave, perhaps military supplies. Quite convenient, was it not? Or that Jesus and the Twelve shared their lunch with the people, and others, inspired by their example, did likewise. But neither of these satisfies the fourfold gospel record. If we accept Jesus as the Son of God, could He not, who by natural laws had made the food in the first place, have multiplied it by higher laws within His knowledge but which are unknown to us?

2. *A Revolutionary Purpose Thwarted* (6:14, 15). Some modern men may question this miracle. But those who witnessed it did not. They said of Jesus, "This is of a truth that prophet that should come into the world" (v. 14). They saw in this miracle that Jesus fulfilled Deuteronomy 18:15, which they interpreted as a Messianic prophecy. Moses had said, "The Lord thy God will raise up unto thee a Prophet from the midst of thee, of thy brethren, like unto me; unto him ye shall hearken."

One can see how they would relate Jesus to this prophecy. Certainly He was a "Prophet." A Galilean, He was "from the midst of thee." He was "of thy brethren," a Jew. His miracle corresponded to Moses feeding the Israelites with manna and quail. So He was "like unto me." Therefore, they *hearkened* unto Him as they sought to "take him by force" to make Him a political king (v. 15). Such was the popular concept of the Messiah. Had they succeeded in their purpose it would have meant a revolution against Rome. It would have been the end of Jesus' spiritual, redemptive mission.

Of course, Jesus speedily ended any such effort. The synoptic gospels report that He first sent away the Twelve, and then dismissed the crowd. This sequence may mean that the disciples were encouraging the people in their purpose. At any rate they were not immune to this concept of the Messiah. Jesus certainly wanted to get them away from this revolutionary excitement. So He sent them away in a boat, and then He went alone to pray.

3. *A Miracle at Sea* (6:16-21). The disciples were rowing their way back to Capernaum. Darkness had settled down upon the sea. Because of a strong wind the sea was rough. This made rowing difficult. So late at night (Matthew and Mark say the "fourth watch," between three and six A.M.) they were only about three miles out to sea, or halfway across.

Suddenly the disciples saw Jesus walking on the water as He drew near the boat. Thinking that they were seeing an apparition, they were frightened. But a word from Jesus (v. 20) allayed their fears as they welcomed Him into the boat. John does not tell about Peter walking on the water (Matthew 14:28ff.). Both Matthew and Mark say that "the wind ceased" immediately. This was a miracle. For had it been a natural phenomenon, the wind would have subsided gradually.

With a quiet sea they soon arrived in Capernaum (v. 21). John does not list details. But Matthew says that in the boat the disciples "worshipped" Jesus, saying, "Of a truth thou art the Son of God" (14:33). They needed this demonstration of Jesus' power. On the previous day probably they had been disappointed that Jesus refused to accede to the revolutionary attempt. But in the boat they were reassured that, while they did not yet understand fully, Jesus was the Son of God.

4. *Feeding Time Again* (6:22-28). The next day the people returned to Capernaum, seeking Jesus. When they found Him He was in the synagogue (v. 59). They asked when He had returned. But Jesus knew that their interest in Him was not a

spiritual one. For they had failed completely to understand the purpose of His miracle. So He said, "Ye seek me, not because ye saw the miracles [signs], but because ye did eat of the loaves, and were filled" (v. 26). They were hungry again, and wanted more food.

In the words "were filled" Jesus drew a meaningful picture. For they render a Greek word which might well be translated "were gorged." In classical Greek it is used to express the idea of a cow filling its stomach, yet never saying, "Thanks," nor asking whence the food came or for what purpose it was given. These people were more concerned about their stomachs than about their souls.

So Jesus challenged them to stop working for food that perished. Instead they should work for that which abides unto everlasting life. It was this which He wanted to give to them. In reply they asked Him what they should do in order to "work the works of God" (v. 28)? However, Jesus gave the conversation a different turn.

5. *The Work of God* (6:29-34). ". . . that ye believe on him whom he hath sent" (v. 29). So Jesus turned the conversation from outward works to inward faith. But the people did not follow Him. Instead, they asked for an outward sign in order that they might believe. They ignored the "sign" of the day before. Now they wanted another. They reminded Jesus that Moses had given their fathers "bread from heaven to eat" (v. 31). Jesus had only multiplied earthly victuals. They wanted to see some floating down from heaven.

But still Jesus sought to lead them from the material to the spiritual. He reminded them that Moses did not give the kind of bread of which He was speaking. Only His Father could give them "the true bread from heaven" (v. 32). The manna gave nourishment, but it did not give life. God proposed to give to them the latter. And this life-giving bread was not material substance, but a living Personality. "For the bread of God is he which cometh down from heaven, and giveth life unto the world" (v. 33). Literally, it "keeps on giving life."

So, like the woman at the well, these people were all in favor of receiving such bread. But, like her, they apparently were not thinking of spiritual life but of perpetual nourishment.

6. *The Bread of Life* (6:35-40). The people had failed utterly to grasp the meaning of Jesus' words. They had demanded "bread from heaven." Very well, they would be offered bread from heaven. But it was quite different bread from that which they

envisioned. Jesus clearly identified Himself as the living Bread or the Bread from heaven. And as such He offered complete satisfaction to all who came to Him in faith. "Hunger" and "thirst" (v. 35) are two of the most demanding of the physical appetites. But they are as nothing when compared to spiritual hunger and thirst. These can be satisfied only in Christ.

However, these people had seen Him and had known His wondrous works. But they had not believed in Him, or had not committed themselves to Him. "All that the Father giveth me shall come to me; and him that cometh to me I will in no wise cast out" (v. 37). He had come to do His Father's will, a will which was that He should lose none who came to Him. Even physical death could not separate them from Him. For God wills that He should raise them from the dead at the last day (v. 39).

These verses (37-39), if taken out of context, could be interpreted to mean that only certain individuals can be saved, namely, those "that the Father giveth me" (v. 37). But that this is not true is seen in verse 40. For here Jesus says, "And this is the will of him that sent me, that every one which seeth the Son, and believeth on him, may [should] have everlasting life . . ." Thus Jesus did not say that some are predestined to be saved and others are predestined to be lost, regardless of what they may do. God has willed certain conditions by which "every one" (all) must be saved. And the Father gives to Jesus all who meet these conditions. The sovereignty of God sets the conditions. But man in his free will may either choose to accept or to reject them. If he does the latter he is responsible for the consequences.

7. *The Murmuring Jews* (6:41-51). Who were these "Jews"? Presumably all of this multitude were Jews by birth. But John suddenly injects this label into his narrative. He had a reason for doing so, for this was his way of referring to the unbelieving Jews. The people had been carrying on a dialogue with Jesus, sometimes in a rather flippant manner. But, even so, they had been talking about how they might believe in Him. However, now they began to buzz among themselves in terms of unbelief. They were no longer talking like the "Galileans" who had followed after Jesus. They were talking like the "Jews" in Jerusalem. So we may see in this sudden use of this term that John is leading up to a climax of avowed unbelief on the part of the people of Galilee.

They murmured at Jesus' claim to be "the bread which came down from heaven" (v. 41). So now they spoke in disbelief. The previous day they had been ready to proclaim Him as their political Messiah, because He was one from their midst, even one of their fellow-Jews. But now they turned these very facts against Him.

"Is not this Jesus, the son of Joseph [so they supposed], whose father and mother we know? how is it then that he saith, I came down from heaven?" (v. 42). A prophet without honor, indeed!

But Jesus silenced their buzzing. "Stop murmuring among yourselves" (v. 43). He reminded them that no man could come to Him except he were drawn of His Father. The approach of the soul to Christ must be initiated by the Father. But instead of yielding to it, these people were resisting it. Those who heard the Father's call and learned of Him came to Jesus. But the response must be a voluntary one. And truly he who believes in Christ "keeps on having everlasting life" (v. 47). Then Jesus reavowed His claim to be the "bread of life" (v. 48). He contrasted this "bread" with "manna." These fathers of these people ate manna for forty years, but they all died — physically. Those who eat this bread from heaven will never die — spiritually.

And then Jesus further identified this "bread" as His "flesh, which I will give for the life of the world" (v. 51). Thus He spoke of how this "bread" will give eternal life. It will be through His death on the cross. The word "for" (*huper*) is the word often used to refer to His substitutionary atonement. He will give His flesh on the cross as a substitute or sacrifice for the death which abides in sinful man, that thereby He may give everlasting life to all who will receive it.

8. *A Civil War Among the Jews* (6:52-65). "The Jews therefore strove among themselves" (v. 52). The word for "strove" originally meant to fight in armed conflict and later to wage a war with words. The latter is the sense here. Evidently some of them were beginning to see the spiritual meaning of what Jesus was saying. Others still took Him literally. So they fought among themselves with their conflicting opinions. These latter asked, "How can this man give us [his] flesh to eat?" (v. 52). "His" is not present in the Greek. Still insisting upon thinking at the physical level, they interpreted Jesus' words as cannibalism.

But He did not turn back from His figure of speech. Instead, He made it stronger as He spoke of eating His flesh and drinking His blood (vv. 53-56). Only as men did this could they have life in Him.

John does not record the actual institution of the Lord's Supper. Some interpreters see this passage as His reference to it.

However, this is to strain a point unduly. Jesus was simply trying to show these people how completely they must become identified with His atoning work, if they were to have the life which He would give.

But still they did not rise to the spiritual level of understanding. "Many of his disciples [not the Twelve, but 'learners'], when they had heard this, said, This is an hard saying; who can hear it?" (v. 60). Hearing this, Jesus asked if His words caused them to stumble. If so, what would they do if they saw Him "ascend up where he was before" (v. 62)? Here He not only referred to His ascension back into heaven whence He had come. He also claimed pre-existence.

But then as if to help them to understand what He had been saying, He added, "It is the spirit that quickeneth [makes alive]; the flesh profiteth nothing: the words that I speak unto you, they are spirit, and they are life" (v. 63). These are the words of God. If the people would understand them, they must rise above the fleshly or physical level. But Jesus noted that some of them did not believe in Him. All of this group is described as "disciples" or pupils (learners), but only those are disciples in truth who believe in Jesus. So for the first time He distinguished between superficial believers and true believers. On the surface men may not always be able to tell the difference. But Jesus "knew from the beginning who they were who believed not" (v. 64). Indeed, He also knew "who should betray him."

The former "who" is an indefinite plural. But the latter one is singular, referring to one definite person. Therefore, one year before His death Jesus indicated that He knew the identity of His betrayer. He saw evidence in Judas which would finally result in this foul deed. In all likelihood Judas himself was not yet aware of this. But Jesus knew.

9. *The Massive Retreat* (6:66). John notes that at this point "many of his disciples went back, and walked no more with him." Literally, they "departed [or deserted] to the rear." These "camp-followers," as A. T. Robertson calls them, could not face the demands of Jesus' words. They were interested only in a political Messiah, and in the loaves and fishes. When Jesus refused to fit into their Messianic pattern, the crowds deserted Him.

This is the very reason why John included the events in Chapter 6 in his gospel. For it marked the turning point in Jesus' ministry. The Galilean multitudes had followed Him with great enthusiasm, while Judea largely had been cold toward Him. But when He made it unmistakably clear that He would not fulfill the role of a nationalistic Messiah, the Galileans for the most part lost interest in Him. Note that "many," not all, left Him. Later in Jerusalem some from Galilee will join in acclaiming Him as the "Son of David" on the occasion of His royal entry into Jerusalem. But even this term carried a highly nationalistic connotation.

10. *The Twelve Tested* (6:67-71). Apparently this grand exodus on the part of the people had made the Twelve restless. So Jesus asked, "Will ye also go away?" (v. 67). But the form of the inquiry indicates that He expected a negative answer.

It was indeed a happy sound for Jesus to hear Peter's reply for the Twelve. "Lord, to whom shall we go? thou hast the words of eternal life" (v. 68). Even if the thought of leaving had crossed their minds, it was soon gone. They did not fully understand Jesus' words. But they had enough discernment to know that they were "the words of eternal life." Furthermore, said Peter, "We believe and are sure [know] that thou art the Christ, the Son of the living God" (v. 69; cf. Matthew 16:16). The verbs "believe" and "know" ("are sure") are both in the perfect tense. This means that they have come to *believe* and *know* (by experience), still *believe* and *know*, and will continue to do so, that Jesus is the Christ, the Son of the living God. They have not yet reasoned through this knowledge, but that which they know is anchored to their faith. And thus anchored, it will grow into a conviction of soul which will survive the crucifixion. Through the Resurrection it will receive assurance, an assurance which they will share with the whole world.

Jesus accepted this confession of faith. It proved the wisdom of His choice when He selected the Twelve. Yet He noted that even one of them was a devil. He was not a devil when Jesus chose him, but he is one now. Thus His general statement of verse 64 was now focused on this little band of intimates. With the perspective of history John notes that Jesus spoke of Judas Iscariot. The fact that he was one of the Twelve makes his deed all the more diabolical (v. 71).

The crowds had deserted Jesus. But His little band remained. Henceforth, and particularly for the next six months, He will concentrate upon preparing them for the terrible ordeal which awaits them at His crucifixion one year hence.

FOR FURTHER STUDY

1. Read the article "Messiah" in Hastings *Dictionary of the Bible*, pp. 607-613. Note especially "The Messiah of the Jewish Literature" and "The Messiah of popular expectation in New

Testament times." Also consult the article in *The Zondervan Pictorial Bible Dictionary.*

2. Compare the revolutionary purpose in John 6:14, 15 with Matthew 4:1-10.
3. List what physical bread does for the body, and compare this list with what Jesus does for the spirit of man.
4. Had you been in the multitude on that day in Capernaum, would you have deserted Jesus or would you have stayed with Him?

CHAPTER 5

The Third Visit To Jerusalem

(THE FEAST OF TABERNACLES)
(John 7:1 - 10:21)

Introduction (7:1)
1. The Feast of Tabernacles (7:2)
2. An Air of Expectancy (7:3-13)
3. Jesus at the Feast (7:14-36)
4. Jesus, the Water of Life (7:37-44)
5. The Report of the Temple Police (7:45-53)
6. The Woman Taken in Adultery (8:1-11)
7. Jesus, the Light of the World (8:12-29)
8. The True Nature of Freedom (8:30-36)
9. The True Seed of Abraham (8:37-59)
10. A Man Born Blind (9:1-5)
11. The Healing of the Blind Man (9:6-12)
12. The Sabbath Question Again (9:13-23)
13. The Pharisees Bested (9:24-34)
14. Spiritual Blindness Healed (9:35-41)
15. The True and the False Shepherds (10:1-18)
16. Confusion Among the Pharisees (10:19-21)

Again we meet John's phrase, "after these things" (v. 1). It involves not only the events in chapter 6, but also the remainder of Jesus' withdrawals during the summer and early fall of A.D. 29. This latter John recognizes when he says that He "kept on walking in Galilee, because he kept on willing not to walk in Judea" ("Jewry," KJV). It is a vivid picture of Jesus' activities during this period. Actually, He spent most of this time outside Galilee (in Syrophoenicia, east of the Sea of Galilee, the region of Caesarea-Philippi and Mt. Hermon), but He returned there periodically for brief visits. His reason for avoiding Judea was the Jews' purpose to kill Him.

1. *The Feast of Tabernacles* (7:2). This was one of the great feasts of the Jews. Sometimes called the Feast of Booths, it commemorated God's care over Israel during her wilderness wanderings when the people dwelt in tents or brush arbors (cf. Matthew 17:4). It was the feast of the latter harvest, late in September, and was a joyful occasion, much like an American Thanksgiving. The feast originally lasted for seven days. But after the Babylonian exile an eighth day of solemn assembly was added (Nehemiah 8:18).

2. *An Air of Expectancy* (7:3-13). Jesus had returned to Galilee from the region of Caesarea-Philippi just prior to this feast. Rejecting His half-brothers' counsel to accompany them to Jerusalem, He later went "in secret," or traveled alone rather than in a caravan (vv. 3-10).

It had been about eighteen months since Jesus had visited Jerusalem. But somehow it was anticipated that He would return for this feast. Therefore, the Jewish rulers "were seeking" Him, asking, "Where is he?" (v. 11) They probably wished to arrest Him. The city itself was buzzing with rumors about Jesus. Some of the people insisted that He was a good man, as attested by His words and works. But others, reflecting the attitude of their rulers, said that He deceived the people. But none of these spoke openly about Him, for they were afraid of these rulers.

3. *Jesus at the Feast* (7:14-36). About the middle of the week Jesus arrived, and soon was found teaching in the temple. Since He had not been taught in one of their schools the Jewish rulers marveled at both the content and method of His teaching. Jesus assured them that He was not self-taught, but had been instructed by God. And if they would practice His teachings, they would know whether or not they were of God or of Himself (vv. 15-18). But they did not even keep the law of Moses, else they would not be trying to kill Him (v. 19). Pilgrims from outside Jerusalem evidently were not aware of this purpose. No one was trying to kill Him at the moment. So His words sounded to them like those of a demonized or insane person. However, Jesus was referring back to His previous visit (chapter 5) when such was the case, and continued to be so (vv. 20-24).

Some of the Jerusalem Jews did know of this murderous purpose. So they were amazed that Jesus now taught openly, and the rulers did nothing about it. Did they know that Jesus was indeed the Christ? However, that could not be. They knew where Jesus came from. And popular belief had it that when the Messiah came, no one would know of His origin. Jesus replied that they knew where He came from, but they did not know who sent Him. Therefore, these Jerusalemites kept seeking to seize Him, but were unsuccessful since Jesus' "hour" had not come (vv. 25-30). However, many of the people (pilgrims?) began to believe on Him. Would even the Christ do greater works than Jesus had done? (v. 31).

When the Pharisees heard of the impression which Jesus was making on the people, they sent temple police to arrest Him (v. 32). Their arrival suggested the night six months hence when they would take Him to be tried and crucified. So to the people Jesus said that for a little while He would be with them, and then would go to "him that sent me" (v. 33). They would seek Him, and not find Him. Failing to understand Him the crowd thought that He might be going to teach Jews outside of Palestine, or even the Greeks (v. 35).

4. *Jesus, the Water of Life* (7:37-44). It was now the last (eighth) day of the feast, the day for the Holy Convocation. On each of the previous seven days the priests had brought, in golden pitchers, water from the pool of Siloam. In the temple this was poured out to commemorate the water which God had provided during Israel's wilderness wanderings, and to remind the Jews of the prophecies concerning the coming of the Spirit of God. As the water was being poured out the singers chanted Isaiah 12:3. "Therefore with joy shall ye draw water out of the wells of salvation." This ceremony was repeated on the eighth day, except that the pitcher contained no water, a reminder that the prophecies had not been fulfilled. Judaism offered no present reality, only a future hope.

At the moment when the empty pitcher was presented, Jesus stood and cried, "If any man thirst, let him come unto me, and drink" (v. 37). The one believing in Him not only shall quench his own thirst, but out of him shall flow rivers of living water to quench the thirst of others (v. 38). John notes that Jesus was speaking of the coming of the Holy Spirit at Pentecost. Through the Holy Spirit in the believer this living water will become a mighty stream.

These words of Jesus produced a division among the people. So there ensued an argument as to whether or not He were the Christ (vv. 40-44).

5. *The Report of the Temple Police* (7:45-53). The officers sent to arrest Jesus returned empty-handed. Their only excuse was that "never man spake like this man" (v. 46). This report enraged the Pharisees. Jesus had even deceived their own police.

Had any of the Sadducees or even the more orthodox Pharisees believed on Him? (vv. 47, 48)

But Jesus had one friend in court, for Nicodemus raised the legal question about condemning Him without hearing Him (v. 49). He had heard Jesus. Whether or not he were yet a believer, at least he was a fair-minded seeker. However, he reaped only scorn for his trouble. He talked like a Galilean, said his colleagues. They challenged him to search and discover that no prophet came out of Galilee. As a matter of fact some had, but prejudice cannot be bothered with the facts.

6. *The Woman Taken in Adultery* (8:1-11). John 7:53 - 8:11 is not found in the oldest and best manuscripts. But it does appear in many of the later ones, beginning in the sixth century A.D. Some place it at the end of John's gospel, and others even have it in Luke. However, it is rather generally agreed that this is a true story from the life of Jesus. And it is with this conviction that it is treated here.

The day following the Feast of Tabernacles some Pharisees brought to Jesus a woman taken in the very act of adultery (vv. 3, 4). According to the Mosaic law she should be stoned to death. But they used her to ensnare Jesus by asking, "But what sayest thou?" (v. 5) If He advised stoning, they could accuse Him of being unmerciful. If He counseled mercy, then He would be going against the law. So, thought they, either way Jesus answered they had Him in a trap.

But He gave neither answer. Instead He stooped down and wrote on the ground. This is the only time He is mentioned as writing. What He wrote no one knows. Then rising up He said, "He that is without sin among you, let him cast a stone at her" (v. 7). He probably meant the same sin of unchastity, either by deed, look, or thought (cf. Matthew 5:28). Then He stooped down and continued to write.

Convicted in their consciences the accusers slipped away, one by one, beginning with the eldest. Arising, Jesus asked the woman, "Hath no man condemned thee?" (v. 10) Literally, "found guilty and pronounced sentence." No man had. So Jesus said, "Neither do I condemn [find guilty and pronounce sentence] thee: go and sin no more" (v. 11). He did not condone her sin, but He gave her another chance. We can only hope that she took it.

7. *Jesus, the Light of the World* (8:12-29). Jesus was in the Court of the Woman in which were located the receptacles for the gifts of the worshipers (v. 21). Each night during the Feast of Tabernacles it was lighted with candelabra, to commemorate the

pillar of fire over the Israelites in the wilderness. Now the lights were extinguished. It was a situation similar to that of the empty pitcher. And Jesus reacted accordingly.

He said, "I am the light of the world: he that followeth me shall not walk in darkness, but shall have the light of life" (v. 12). This statement prompted the Pharisees to question His authority to bear such a witness. But Jesus replied that according to the Mosaic code the testimony of two men is true. And both He and His Father bore witness of Him (vv. 13-18). In the course of this debate Jesus alluded to His death and Resurrection, and plainly said that the Pharisees would help to bring Him to His death (vv. 21-29).

8. *The True Nature of Freedom* (8:30-36). Some of the Pharisees *began to believe* on Jesus (v. 30). And He reminded them that if their faith were genuine, they would know the truth which would make them free. Proudly the Pharisees claimed to be Abraham's seed, and that they never had, were not then, and never would be in bondage to any man (v. 33). This strong statement is involved in the verb form which they used. They had been in bondage many times. Ironically at that very moment they were the vassals of Rome. But Jesus spoke of bondage to sin. From that, "if the Son therefore shall make you free, ye shall be free indeed" (v. 36).

9. *The True Seed of Abraham* (8:37-59). The Pharisees claimed to be Abraham's seed. Yet they were seeking to kill Jesus because He had spoken the truth of God. This Abraham did not do (vv. 37-40). So Jesus said that they were doing the deeds of their father, the devil. The Pharisees' only reply was to slander His parentage, as they supposed, and to claim God as their Father (v. 41). But Jesus reavowed their diabolical parentage (v. 44). Their father, the devil, was a murderer from the beginning, a liar, and the father of lies. Proof that they are not God's children is their attitude toward Jesus (vv. 45-50).

But any man who keeps Jesus' teaching will never see death (v. 51). The Pharisees ridiculed Him all the more, reminding Him that both Abraham and the prophets kept God's word, yet they were all dead. So they asked Jesus if He were greater than Abraham and the prophets.

The Pharisees claimed Abraham as their father. Very well. But Abraham saw Messiah's day (in prospect), and rejoiced. They saw it in fact, and were angry. In turn they reminded Jesus that He was under fifty years of age (actually thirty-three). So "hast thou seen Abraham?" (v. 57) But He claimed eternal, essential being as He said, "Before Abraham was, I am" (v. 58). Literally, "before Abraham came into being, I always am." This means that Jesus claimed oneness with God. The Pharisees so understood Him, as seen by their effort to stone Him. But He simply left the temple, as they stood with stones in their hands.

10. *A Man Born Blind* (9:1-5). As Jesus went along He saw a man who was blind from birth. To the disciples the man posed a theological problem. "Master, who did sin, this man, or his parents, that he was born blind?" (v. 2) A baby sinning before birth? To them a given sickness was due to a given sin. It may be true, but not necessarily so.

But to Jesus the man was an opportunity. He strictly denied the theological assumption of the disciples. Then He made a puzzling statement, "But that the works of God should be made manifest in him" (v. 3). Was he born blind for this purpose? Such is hardly in keeping with the character of God. The original Greek version of this had no punctuation. This was furnished by the translators. So we are justified in furnishing our own. "Neither this man, nor his parents. But that the works of God should be made manifest in him, I must work the works of him that sent me, while it is day: the night cometh when no man can work" (vv. 3, 4). This is in keeping with the character and purpose of God, and with the ministry of Jesus. God's work is not to make men blind, but to give sight. So Jesus worked the works of God when He healed him (v. 5).

11. *The Healing of the Blind Man* (9:6-12). Jesus "spat" on the ground, made spittle, and with it anointed the man's eyes. The Greek word for "spat" is *ptuo*. Its very sound suggests the act of spitting. The Jews held that saliva was useful in treating eye-trouble. Jesus did not so believe, as is seen in the fact that He did not use it in other cases of blindness. Here He accommodated Himself to this belief as an aid to the man's faith.

The man did as Jesus told him. He washed his eyes in the pool of Siloam, and returned seeing. He was a well-known beggar. People asked what had happened to him, and he told them (vv. 8-11). But he could not tell them where Jesus was. So they brought him to the Pharisees.

12. *The Sabbath Question Again* (9:13-23). The Pharisees' concern here as in chapter 5 was the fact that this healing had occurred on the Sabbath. Obviously the one who did it was not of God, said some. But others questioned how a sinner could heal blindness. Their only out was to question the man's blindness at all. So they called his parents, who affirmed that he had been

born blind. However, they were reluctant to say more lest they should be turned out of the synagogue (vv. 21, 22). (This was something akin to excommunication today.) So they said of their son, "He is of age; ask him" (v. 23). After all, he was the one who was healed. If anyone is to be excommunicated, let it be he. Some parents!

13. *The Pharisees Bested* (9:24-34). They were past masters in debate, but the Pharisees more than met their match in this clever man. Said they to him, "Give God the praise: we know that this man is a sinner" (v. 24). "Give God the praise" was their way of putting the man on oath to tell the truth. The man replied that he was not qualified to judge whether or not Jesus was a sinner. He only knew that "whereas I was blind, now I see" (v. 25). The testimony of an experience!

When the Pharisees pressed him further to explain his experience, the man taunted them (vv. 26-29). He had already told them. Now they want to hear it again. Were they interested in becoming Jesus' disciples? But in reply they claimed to be Moses' disciples. "As for this fellow, we know not from whence he is" (v. 29).

And then the man taught the teachers. They were supposed to know everything. Yet this man opened his eyes, and they did not know about Him. "Now we know [Note the 'we'. He associated himself with the scholars.] that God heareth not sinners [They said, 'Amen.'] . . . since the world began was it not heard that any man opened the eyes of one that was born blind. If this man were not of God, he could do nothing" (vv. 31-33). There were no "amens" here. School was out as the unwilling pupils ran off their upstart teacher! (v. 34). But they did not cast him out of the synagogue.

14. *Spiritual Blindness Healed* (9:35-41). Jesus later found the man and healed his spiritual blindness. He believed on Jesus as the Son of God (vv. 35-38). As for the Pharisees, they remained spiritually blind, because they willed not to see. And for that reason they were responsible for their sin (v. 41).

15. *The True and the False Shepherds* (10:1-18). Jesus used this occasion to distinguish between the true and false shepherds, or between Himself and the Pharisees.

Therefore, He spoke the *allegory* of the Good Shepherd. The word rendered "parable" in verse 6 means *a wayside saying.* The word for parable *(parabole)* does not appear in John. A parable usually teaches one point, with little emphasis being placed on the details of the story. An allegory is a kind of parable in that it also stresses one theme. But it approaches it from many angles through the details. So in the allegory of the Good Shepherd Jesus drew many pictures of the Pharisees and other false shepherds in contrast to Himself.

First, let us notice the allegory (vv. 1-5). A thief and a robber are those who climb over the wall of the sheepfold. A shepherd enters through the door. Since he has a right to enter, the doorkeeper opens the door for him. A shepherd names his sheep, and they know his voice. Even though many flocks at night may stay in one community fold, in the morning a given shepherd's sheep follow him out of the fold because they know his voice. They will not follow a strange shepherd.

Second, let us follow Jesus' application of the allegory (vv. 7-18). He identified Himself as "the door" of the sheep. Not "a door" among many doors, but the only door into the spiritual fold of God. Any shepherd who does not enter by this door is a false shepherd. Said Jesus, "All that ever came before me are thieves and robbers: but the [true] sheep did not hear them" (v. 8). This reference is to false messiahs, false prophets, and false teachers. But Jesus is "the door" through which men may enter into God's fold, be saved, and have access to both safety and pasture (v. 9). Thieves come for but one purpose: to satisfy their own fleshly desires. To do this they will steal, and if necessary, kill and destroy. But Jesus is the "good" or "beautiful" Shepherd, beautiful in both character and service. He is come to give life in abundance. And He will do so by giving His life "for [as a substitute for] the sheep" (v. 11).

Then Jesus turned to the Pharisees themselves. They were not true shepherds, but *hirelings.* They were only timeservers_whose sole interest in the sheep was what they could get out of the animals for themselves (vv. 12, 13). Not owning the sheep, when the wolves come they will look out for "Number One." So they ran away, leaving the sheep to be ravaged by the wolves. But Jesus, "the good shepherd," lays down His life to save His sheep.

Furthermore, Jesus said that His "fold" includes other sheep than those among the Jews. Thus He looked beyond the borders of Palestine to those whom He will redeem to God by His blood "out of every kindred, and tongue, and people, and nation" (Revelation 5:9). And this He will do by laying down His life and taking it up again, namely, through His death and Resurrection (v. 17). No man will take His life from Him. He will lay it down voluntarily, and take it up again, by the expressed will and mighty power of His Father.

16. *Confusion Among the Pharisees* (10:19-21). Heretofore Jesus' words had produced a schism among the people (7:12, 31, 43). Now the Pharisees themselves were divided. Many of them said that Jesus was demon-possessed and insane. Why listen to Him? But others said, "These are not the words of him that hath a devil. Can a devil open the eyes of the blind?" (v. 21)

But none are so blind as those who will not to see.

FOR FURTHER STUDY

1. Read "Feast of Tabernacles" in Hastings *Dictionary of the Bible,* p. 888. Also see the article in *The Zondervan Pictorial Bible Dictionary.*
2. Make a list of the things that water does for the body, and compare them with what Jesus does for the human spirit.
3. Repeat the same process concerning "light."
4. The healed blind man answered the skeptics by relating his *experience.* Share your experience in Christ with an unbeliever.
5. In the light of the allegory of the Good Shepherd read Psalm 23, Luke 15:4-7; John 21:15-17; Hebrews 13:20, 21; I Peter 5:1-4.

CHAPTER 6

The Fourth Visit To Jerusalem

(THE FEAST OF DEDICATION)
(John 10:22-42)

Introduction
1. The Feast of Dedication (10:22)
2. A Demand for Clear Identity (10:23-30)
3. The Reaction of the Jews (10:31-33)
4. Jesus' Claim Tested by Scripture (10:34-39)
5. Jesus Goes Beyond the Jordan (10:40-42)

A period of approximately three months intervenes between John 10:21 and John 10:22. During this interval Jesus had been engaged in a ministry outside of Jerusalem but confined to Judea (cf. Luke 10:1 - 13:21). At the end of this period He returned to Jerusalem for the Feast of Dedication. John notes that "it was winter" (v. 22). Actually, it was about the middle of December, A.D. 29.

1. *The Feast of Dedication* (10:22). This feast, which lasted eight days, commemorated the cleansing and rededication of the temple by Judas Maccabeus in 164 B.C. Antiochus Epiphanes, the Seleucid ruler of Syria, sought to impose Greek customs and religion on the Jews. He met opposition especially in Judea. As a result he inflicted many atrocities upon the Jewish people. His crowning act in this regard was to desecrate the holy temple. He reconstructed it in honor of Zeus Olympius, erected a pagan altar upon the altar of burnt-offering, and sacrificed swine thereon. He also introduced the heathen ritual with all of its evil practices. Finally, the Jews revolted against him. Following their

victory under Judas Maccabeus, they once again cleansed and dedicated the temple to the worship of Jehovah.

Even though the Feast of Dedication was not one of the greater feasts among the Jews, it was one of the most joyous. It was also called the Feast of Lights, since one of its features was to have the private homes brilliantly lighted. For the most part the Jews celebrated it in the synagogues of their own cities or villages. But since Jesus was already in Judea, He journeyed to Jerusalem for its observance.

2. *A Demand for Clear Identity* (10:23-30). Sometime during the week of this feast Jesus was walking along Solomon's porch in the temple area. This was a covered colonnade which ran along the eastern edge of the temple. It afforded protection in any kind of weather.

Suddenly He was encircled by a group of the hostile Jewish rulers. They were still angered by His stinging words spoken to them three months earlier. So they said, "How long dost thou make us to doubt?" (v. 24) Actually, "to hold us in suspense?" Repeatedly in the past they had tried to get Him to tell them who He was (cf. 8:25). But always He replied in language which they could not twist into an accusation concerning Him. Therefore, they challenged Him to come to the point. "If thou be the Christ, tell us plainly" (v. 24). For the sake of argument they assumed that He was the Christ. But the point of their demand was for Him to say so "plainly." They wanted Him to say flatly, "I am the Christ."

Jesus had avoided using this title when speaking to the Jewish leaders, His reason being that they attached to it a highly nationalistic sense. At times without protest He permitted others to call Him "the Christ." Near Caesarea-Philippi He had sought such a declaration from the Twelve, and rejoiced when they gave it. To the Samaritan woman He admitted to being such. Finally, under oath He would confess to being the Christ, the Son of God (Matthew 26:63f.). When He did so, the Sanhedrin voted Him to be guilty of blasphemy, and before Pilate charged Him with being a king. So knowing the purpose of the Jewish rulers, He had refused to make this claim "plainly" before them. He will not do so until the right moment in God's time-table. But His hour had not yet come.

Rather than to say plainly, "I am the Christ," Jesus reminded them that He had told them who He was. His works had given testimony that He was God's Son. But they had believed neither His words nor His works. This was because they were not His sheep, as He had told them three months before (10:4). His sheep hear and heed His voice, He knows them, and they follow Him.

Furthermore, He gives unto them eternal life. "And they shall never perish, neither shall any [one] pluck [snatch] them out of my hand" (v. 28). "Never" renders a strong, emphatic double negative. In English two negatives make a positive. But in Greek two negatives make a stronger negative. So Jesus emphatically said that His sheep shall "not never" be destroyed. The word rendered "perish" is the verb from which comes the word Apollyon, the destroyer, one name for the devil. And in this light the absence of "man" from the Greek text takes on added meaning. Actually, "no one," neither man nor devil, shall snatch Jesus' sheep out of His hand.

And, in addition, He said, "My Father, which gave them me, is greater than all; and no [one] is able to pluck [snatch] them out of my Father's hand" (v. 29). Here is security par excellence. This security rests not in the believer's ability to hold on to God in Christ. It is the ability of the Father and the Son to hold on to the believer. Many will try to snatch them away. But they must defeat God Himself in order to do so!

The Jews had asked Jesus to tell them "plainly" who He was. Very well. He would tell them. Not by using their prescribed word, which they could use against Him. But He made an even greater claim than they asked. "I and my [the] Father are one" (v. 30). He did not say, "The Father and I are one." He put the "I" before "the Father." Not that He is greater than the Father. But the "I" is in the emphatic position. The Jews had demanded that He identify Himself "plainly." He could not have made it any plainer. "I and the Father *are one*" (author's italics). One in nature. One in essence. One in eternal, essential being. Two persons, but one nature. In truth Jesus said, "I am God."

Jesus had repeatedly spoken of the relation between Father and Son. This declaration is the acme of them all. "Plainly," it is not only "the Father" and "the Son." The Son and the Father are one.

3. *The Reaction of the Jews* (10:31-33). This clearest of all Jesus' claims to deity sent the Jews into a rage beyond their control. They "took up stones again to stone him" (v. 31). The "again" refers back to John 8:59. But there is one difference between these two verses. Two different words are used for "took up." In 8:59 the word suggests that they merely picked up stones that were handy. But A. T. Robertson suggests that the word used in 10:31 probably means that "they fetched stones from a distance."

They picked them up and bore them. There were probably no stones on Solomon's porch. The suggestion is that in the former instance, the Jews acted through impulsive anger. But in the latter they were so enraged that they went out and found stones, bent upon making a final end of this one whom they regarded as an arch-blasphemer.

But Jesus stood His ground before this enraged and murderous group. He reminded them that they had seen Him perform many *good* works "from my Father." "For which of those works do ye stone me?" (v. 32) Literally, "Are ye trying to stone me?" Evidently they had already drawn back their arms, ready to cast their stones.

They replied that they were not stoning Him for any good work, but for "blasphemy" (v. 33). This is the only time that this word appears in John's gospel. Their reason for stoning Jesus was that "thou, being a man, makest thyself God" (v. 33). In John 5:18 they sought to kill Jesus because He made Himself "equal with God." But here they said that He *made Himself God.*

There are those who insist that Jesus never claimed to be God. But the Jews so understood Him here. And the language justifies their understanding. There is no question but that He made Himself God. The question is whether or not He blasphemed in doing so. If He and the Father are not one, then He did. But if they are one, He did not speak evil but the truth. The testimony of the Scriptures, plus the testimony of history, plus the testimony of the personal experience of all who have believed in Him avow that He spoke the truth.

4. *Jesus' Claim Tested by Scripture* (10:34-39). The Jews who accused Jesus of blasphemy had neither history after the event nor a personal experience of faith by which to test His claim. But they did have the Old Testament Scriptures. And they insisted that they were their divinely appointed interpreters. So taking them at their word, Jesus referred to Psalm 82:6 to refute their charge of blasphemy.

The judges of Israel had been corrupt in their office. And God reproved them for it. In the psalm God is represented as calling them "gods," because they are His representatives. "I said, Ye are gods." He did not say, "Ye are Jehovahs," or equal to the true God of Israel. But "Ye are *Elohim*," which was the general term for any god. However, it was used to refer to Israel's God also. In Greek this word was rendered as *Theos* or *theos*, the one word for God or god. It was this word that John uses where the Jews said of Jesus, "makest thyself God."

Now, Jesus said, "If he called them gods [*theoi*], unto whom the word of God came . . . ." This was their only claim to being "gods." And then, parenthetically, He reminded His critics that "the scriptures cannot be broken." The Pharisees would have to accept this as true. So, in effect, Jesus said that He was quoting God's abiding Word to them.

And then He drove home His point. If the above be true why was it that of Him, whom God sanctified and sent into the world, they said, "Thou blasphemeth," because He said, "I am the Son of God" (v. 36)? They could not be true to their own Scriptures and so charge Him. So once again Jesus had silenced them.

On the basis of these words some insist that Jesus never really claimed deity. They hold that He simply put Himself on the same level with the judges under consideration in Psalm 82:6. To be sure, as A. T. Robertson points out in defending Jesus' claim to deity, He did not call Himself the "Son of Jahweh" or Jehovah. He said that He is "a Son of God" or of *Theos*. (The definite article does not appear in the best manuscripts.) And as Robertson further holds, this "can mean only 'Son of *Elohim*.'" (*Word Pictures*, in loco). But to say that by this Jesus disclaimed deity is to shrink His meaning in an unmerited fashion. As noted above, the Greek language had only one word for God (*Theos*). And in this passage Jesus only used this play on words to answer His accusers. The author agrees with Robertson's conclusion. Jesus "is simply stopping the mouths of the rabbis from the charge of blasphemy and he does it effectively" (*Ibid*, in loco).

That His claim to deity went beyond that of Psalm 82 is clearly seen in Jesus' words which followed. "If I do not the works of my Father, believe me not" (v. 37). He was willing to stake His claim to deity on His works. They might deny catigorically His words. But His works stood for themselves. Words of denial could not alter the facts of a man walking who had been crippled for thirty-eight years or of one born blind who now saw.

"But if I do [the works of my Father], though ye believe not me, believe the works" (v. 38). The Greek is much more meaningful than the English version. "Though ye keep on not believing me, keep on believing the works: in order that ye may come to know, and keep on knowing, that the father is in me, and I in the Father." Here is oneness. Literally, "in me the Father, and I in the Father." This is tantamount to Jesus' claim in verse 30. "I and the Father are one." So Jesus closed the conversation by reaffirming His oneness with the Father or His deity. And this in spite of the fact that the Jews stood with their stones poised to crush Him to death.

Evidently they cast aside their stones. But they kept on seeking to seize Him. However, Jesus walked from the field of conflict the victor. And He left behind Him an angry, confused, but resolute foe.

5. *Jesus Goes Beyond the Jordan* (10:40-42). It was quite certain that the Jewish rulers would never believe the claims of Jesus. In fact with each of His succeeding visits to Jerusalem, this became more evident. The recent violent episode saw the line of battle drawn more tightly than ever. But for Jesus' dominant personality and unanswerable logic, already they might have killed Him in a scene of mob violence. And His hour had not yet come. So He left Jerusalem, to return to the city no more until He came for the final showdown.

Therefore, with His disciples He journeyed eastward to the place beyond the Jordan River where John the Baptist had preached and baptized (v. 40). There He remained for some time. John notes that great crowds came to Him. This was in Perea. And even though the Galilean multitudes had long since forsaken Him, the people of Perea flocked about Him.

This seems to be John's summary of the Perean ministry that is recorded more fully in Luke 13:22 - 16:10. But in keeping with his supplementary purpose, John only touches upon it in preparation for that which he records in chapter 11.

However, he adds one interesting note which is not found in Luke, but which explains the effectiveness of the Perean ministry which Luke does record. The people who came to Jesus there said "John [the Baptist] did no miracle [sign]: but all things that John spoke of this man were true" (v. 41). What a compliment they paid to the Baptist's preaching! He had long since been beheaded by Herod Antipas. His eloquent tongue had been silenced. But his work lived on after him. He performed no "sign" by which to authenticate his message. But he had so faithfully portrayed the Christ that when Jesus appeared among them, they recognized Him. Thus Jesus Himself was the Baptist's "sign" that he was a man sent from God.

John the Baptist had *decreased* indeed. But Christ had *increased*. And the friend of the Bridegroom wished it to be so. The Bridegroom continued to increase in Perea as "many believed on him there" (v. 42).

What satisfaction and honor any preacher or Christian teacher should have to know that John 10:41, 42 would be his fitting epitaph! Who among them would want any less?

FOR FURTHER STUDY

1. In order to understand the background of the Feast of Dedication, in Hastings *Dictionary of the Bible* read the articles on Antiochus Epiphanes (p. 38), Mattathias and Judas Maccabeus (p. 562), and the Feast of Dedication, (p. 184).
2. In His words, "I and the Father are one" (John 10:30), Jesus claimed deity. From memory make your own list of ways in which Jesus revealed the Father.
3. Why did the Jews undertake to stone Jesus to death on this occasion? See John 10:33.
4. What was the greatest element in the preaching of John the Baptist: zeal, eloquence, fearlessness, Scriptural content, intelligence, or that it revealed Jesus Christ to His hearers?
5. How can you help others to see Jesus in you?

CHAPTER 7

The Raising Of Lazarus

(John 11:1-54)

Introduction
1. A Crisis in Bethany (11:1-4)
2. The Strange Reaction of Jesus (11:5-16)
3. Jesus' Reception in Bethany (11:17-37)
4. Lazarus Come Forth (11:38-44)
5. The Reaction to the "Sign" (11:45-53)
6. The Reaction of Jesus (11:54)

Jesus' Perean ministry was interrupted by a visit to Bethany, a village located about two miles from Jerusalem on the southeastern slopes of the Mount of Olives. Here lived the family of Lazarus, and his sisters, Mary and Martha. Luke records a previous visit of Jesus to their home. In all likelihood He had made, and would make, other such visits.

1. *A Crisis in Bethany* (11:1-4). So his sisters sent word to Jesus, "Lord, behold, the one whom thou lovest is sick" (v. 3). The fact that they sent for Jesus indicates how serious his illness was.

But when Jesus heard the news, He told the messenger and His disciples that it was not a sickness unto final death. By it both the Father and the Son would receive glory. In his mystical way John records this to intimate that the events connected with this illness would be related to His death on the cross, through which Jesus would receive His greatest glory.

2. *The Strange Reaction of Jesus* (11:5-16). Even though Jesus loved these people, He did not respond immediately to their need. Instead, He remained in Perea for two days. Such an action must have seemed strange to His friends then, even as it does to us until we read the entire story. For obviously He waited until Lazarus was dead. In fact, Lazarus probably was dead, or

very near death, at the moment when Jesus heard about his illness. At that time He was about two or three days' travel from
Bethany.

Finally, Jesus announced to His disciples His purpose to
return to Judea. Remembering the murderous purpose of the
Jewish rulers, the disciples advised otherwise. In somewhat vague
language Jesus replied that His enemies could not accomplish their
purpose until His "hour" had come (vv. 9, 10). And then He
said, "Our friend Lazarus sleepeth; but I must go, that I may
awake him out of sleep" (v. 11). Interpreting the word "sleep"
in the natural sense, they observed that Lazarus must be improving.
Then Jesus said plainly, "Lazarus is dead" (v. 14). Furthermore,
He was glad for their sakes that He was not there to heal him.
For as the result of the death of Lazarus, they would have an additional reason to believe in Him.

When Jesus insisted on going, Thomas, one of the Twelve,
said to the others, "Let us also go, that we may die with him"
(v. 16). We can admire this heroic loyalty on the part of Thomas,
and of the others, for they went with Jesus even though they
thought that they were facing certain death in doing so.

3. *Jesus' Reception in Bethany* (11:17-37). When Jesus arrived in Bethany, He found that Lazarus had been entombed for
four days. Many Jews from Jerusalem had come to the home to
mourn with and to bring comfort to the bereaved sisters. Martha,
hearing that Jesus was coming, went out to meet Him. But Mary,
probably prostrated with grief, remained in the house. Martha,
ever the practical one, was probably busy looking after her guests.
Even though deep sorrow possessed her, life still must go on.

When Martha met Jesus, she said, "Lord, if thou hadst been
here, my brother had not died" (v. 21). Her words contained
a mingled faith and rebuke. The latter indicates the intimate
friendship between Jesus and these friends. But even though the
sister was bereaved, and somewhat disappointed in Jesus, she still
had hope that whatever He should ask of God, God would grant
it (v. 22). Was this a veiled request that Jesus would even now restore her brother to life?

Jesus assured her that her brother would rise again. She took
Him to refer to the final resurrection. Even though she believed
in this, it did not relieve entirely her present sorrow. And then
Jesus spoke words which were to her, and to all bereaved since,
a source of infinite strength when He said, "I am the resurrection,
and the life: he that believeth in me, though he were dead, yet

shall he live: and whosoever liveth and believeth in me shall never die" (vv. 25, 26). But did Martha really believe this?

Her response was the greatest confession of faith in Jesus as the Messiah which is recorded in the gospels. Yes, even greater than that of Peter (Matthew 16:16). For he made his confession from the pinnacle of exhilaration, as the climax of having viewed a long series of mighty works performed by Jesus. But Martha made hers from the pit of despair. She had sent for Jesus in her hour of great need. Insofar as she could tell, He had failed her. Yet she still believed in Him. Hear her confession. "Yea, Lord: I believe that thou art the Christ, the Son of God, which should come into the world" (v. 27). "Believe" is a verb form meaning "I have believed in the past, still believe, and will continue to believe." She had this faith in the sunshine; she still had it in the dark shadows; she would continue to have it in the future regardless of what might happen. Luke tells us that Martha was a practical woman. Now John tells us that she also was a woman with a tremendous and rugged faith. These two natures are not necessarily incompatible.

Having spoken thusly, Martha went to fetch her sister. By this time they had arrived at the house. So when Mary heard that Jesus was there, she ran and fell at His feet. Then she repeated the words which she and Martha had probably said to each other. "Lord, if thou hadst been here, my brother had not died" (v. 32). But she did not add Martha's words of hope. She believed that Jesus could have healed her brother. But beyond that her hope did not go.

Jesus' own emotions were caught up in this scene of mourning (v. 33). So as they were going toward the tomb, "Jesus wept" (v. 35). Literally, "Jesus burst into tears." His human sympathy entered freely into the sorrow of Martha and Mary.

But even in this tender scene unbelief raised its hydra head. Some of the Jews noted how much Jesus loved Lazarus. But others asked, "Could not this man, which opened the eyes of the blind, have caused that even this man should not have died?" (v. 37)

4. *Lazarus Come Forth* (11:38-44). By this time they had arrived at the tomb. It was a cave over the entrance of which had been placed a stone for the purpose of keeping out wild animals. This was a common mode of burial. Modern tourists are shown such a cave, reported to be the one in which Lazarus was buried.

Jesus told them to remove the stone. This much man could

do. But Martha protested that Lazarus' body was already decaying, since he had been dead four days. There was a tradition among the Jews that after death the soul hovers about the body for three days, hoping to re-enter it. But on the fourth day it leaves it. There is no evidence in Martha's protest that she believed this. Hers was a natural concern about a decaying body. But this tradition may furnish a clue as to why Jesus had waited until the fourth day after Lazarus' death. There must be no superstitious question about what He was about to do. It must be an unquestioned "sign" of His deity, and His lordship over death.

So with a mild rebuke to Martha (v. 40), Jesus waited until the stone was removed. Then after a prayer of thanksgiving to the Father for answering His prayer even before He prayed it, Jesus spoke. With a loud voice He cried, "Lazarus, come forth " (v. 43). This "great [elevated] voice" was not for Lazarus' benefit. Jesus wanted all present to hear, and to see that Lazarus responded simultaneously with His call. And he came forth, bound in his graveclothes in the manner used in Jewish and other ancient burials. Then Jesus once again called upon man to do what man could do. "Loose him, and let him go" (v. 44). Those who were present had viewed the greatest of Jesus' "signs."

Was this a resurrection in the usual sense of that word? Hardly so. For Jesus Himself was the "firstfruits" out of the realm of the dead (I Corinthians 15:20). "Resurrection" means to come to life again to die no more. That which happened to Lazarus was more of a *resusitation*. He who was truly dead was restored to life again, but his body once more would die. Thereafter, he will be raised in the final resurrection to die no more.

5. *The Reaction to the "Sign"* (11:45-53). One might think that all who saw Jesus raise Lazarus from the dead would have believed in Him as the Son of God. And many did so. But others of them rushed back to Jerusalem to report the event to the Pharisees. Knowing the Pharisees' belief in the resurrection, we might also expect them to be delighted with the news. However, they were so committed in their opposition to Jesus that they simply reported the matter to the chief priests, Sadducees who did not believe in the resurrection from the dead.

At this point we begin to discern John's purpose in recording the raising of Lazarus. This event fully demonstrated that Jesus was Lord over death. The synoptic gospels had recorded two previous raisings from the dead by Jesus. But they had occurred in Galilee. Now He had raised Lazarus within two miles of the Jewish temple, the seat of Sadducean power. Jews from Jerusalem had

seen it. And many others would go to Bethany to see this man
who had been raised from the dead by Jesus (12:10, 11). Reports
from Galilee about such matters the Sadducees could deny as being the idle stories of simple people. But they could not deny
the raising of Lazarus. So, in essence, Jesus had thrown down the
gauntlet to them at their most sensitive spot. And this almost
within the shadow of the temple!

And they took it up immediately. They called the Sanhedrin
into session in order to deal with Him. Up to this point the major
opposition to Jesus had been left up to the Pharisees, with an occa-
sional assist from the Sadducees. But from this time on the Sadducees assume charge. It is a debatable question as to whether or
not the Pharisees alone ever would have put Jesus to death. They
might have argued and worried Him to death, but nothing more.
However, the Sadducees were realists. They wasted little time in
argument. So when Jesus dared to challenge them directly, from
the human standpoint His doom was sealed.

When the Sanhedrin was assembled, a general discussion ensued. "What do we?" or, literally, "What are we doing? for this
man keeps on doing many signs" (v. 47). (And from the standpoint of the Sadducees the most recent one was the most unforgive-
able.) This sounds like an accusation of the Sadducees against the
Pharisees. The latter had been doing plenty, but with no apparent
results. And then they revealed their true reason for opposing
Jesus. If they let Jesus alone, all men would believe on Him.
"And the Romans shall come, and take away our place and nation"
(v. 48). Notice that they put "place" before "nation." Jesus was
a threat to their places of power among the Jews. The Pharisees
were opposed to Roman rule. But they posed as the teachers of
Israel. The people were leaving them to follow this unaccredited
teacher from Nazareth. The Sadducees, on the other hand, were
perfectly willing for the Roman rule to continue, so long as they
were permitted by the Romans to enjoy a certain amount of ruling power and to grow wealthier thereby.

But Jesus was a threat to the privileges and power of both
groups. If things continued as they were now going, they foresaw
a revolution against Rome. Such could have but one end. A defeat by the Romans, and with it the loss of their "place and nation."

This general discussion was getting them nowhere. So Caiaphas,
the high priest, took charge. Said he, "Ye know nothing at all."
This was certainly true insofar as any solution to their problem
was concerned. And then he made a definite proposal. "It is ex-
pedient [profitable] for us, that one man should die for [*huper*,

as a substitute] the people, and that the whole nation perish not"
or "may not be destroyed" (v. 50). It was as simple as that.
Either Jesus must die, or the nation, including them, would be
destroyed. And it was to their profit that the former should happen. Therefore, the entire matter was to be decided, not on what
was right, but on the basis of expediency.

John inserts a parenthetical statement at this point. He notes
that Caiaphas did not say this of himself. He did not really know
what he was saying. "But being high priest that year, he prophesied that Jesus should die for that nation; and not for that nation
only, but that also he should gather together in one the children of
God that were scattered abroad" (vv. 51, 52). This, of course, is
John's interpretation *after the fact*. Unknowingly Caiaphas had
prophesied *the substitutionary atonement*. He had predicted how
Jesus would die — as a Substitute. However, he had no knowledge
of or interest in such matters. He simply made a grim proposal
as to how the members of the Sanhedrin might save their own
skins. But God had an overruling purpose for it all.

So the time for voting had arrived. And the question before
them was, to their way of thinking, quite simple, Either they could
go on doing nothing and lose everything in the process, or they
could bring Jesus to His death. It was their loss *versus* Jesus'
death. And they voted for Jesus' death.

We may safely conclude that Nicodemus and Joseph of
Arimathea were absent from this meeting. Nicodemus had shown
previously that he had a sympathy for Jesus (7:50-52); and Luke
clearly implies that Joseph of Arimathea was absent from the session of the Sanhedrin which voted Jesus to be guilty of death
(23:51). The two men were associated together in Jesus' burial.
In all likelihood Caiaphas, knowing of their secret discipleship,
did not call them to attend the meeting.

But from that day forward the Sanhedrin took counsel among
themselves to put Jesus to death (v. 53). They had often purposed
to do it in the past. The Pharisees on more than one occasion
had been on the verge of stoning Him. Now, however, following
the raising of Lazarus, it became the avowed program of the Sanhedrin, the official ruling body among the Jews.

6. *The Reaction of Jesus* (11:54). Evidently Jesus heard of
the resolve of the Sanhedrin. At least John implies this when he
says, "Jesus *therefore* walked no more openly among the Jews"
(author's italics). He did not fear death. But He would not take
undue chances with His life. He had an "hour." But until that
hour should come, He kept out of the way of His designing enemies.

Leaving the immediate vicinity of Jerusalem, therefore, He went into the hill country not far from the Judean wilderness. The location of the village of Ephraim, to which He went, is not known for certain. This is its only mention in the New Testament. But since it was "near to the wilderness," it must have been somewhere northeast of Jerusalem. This was a sparsely settled area, and would provide Jesus with an ideal retreat until He was ready to travel northward into Galilee. From there He will travel in a caravan bound for Jerusalem and the Passover. His "hour" was only a few weeks away.

FOR FURTHER STUDY

1. Read Luke 10:38-42 which records a previous visit of Jesus to the home of Mary and Martha. Compare this picture of Martha with the one in John 11. Read also John 12:1-11.
2. Refer to a map of Palestine in Jesus' day to fix in your mind the location of Bethany with respect to both Jerusalem and Perea.
3. What is the shortest verse in the Bible? Cf. John 11:35. Meditate upon its depth in respect to its length.
4. Read articles on "Mourning Customs" (pp. 635, 636) and "Tomb, Grave, Sepulchre" (p. 942) in Hastings *Dictionary of the Bible* and in *The Zondervan Pictorial Bible Dictionary*.
5. What was the relationship between the raising of Lazarus and the death of Jesus?

CHAPTER 8

The Last Visit To Jerusalem

(THE FOURTH PASSOVER)
(John 11:55 - 12:50)

Introduction (11:55-57)
1. Six Days Before the Passover (12:1, 9-11)
2. The Royal Entry (12:12-19)
3. The Visit of Certain Greeks (12:20-33)
4. A Question and an Answer (12:34-36)
5. John's Commentary Upon Jesus' Words (12:37-43)
6. John's Conclusion of Jesus' Public Ministry (12:44-50)
7. A Supper in Bethany (12:2-8)
8. A Study in Contrasts (12:3, 4)

It was only a few days before the Passover in A.D. 30. Many people began arriving at Jerusalem early in order to purify themselves before the feast began. The principal topic of conversation among them was whether or not Jesus would attend this feast. Word had gotten around that the Sanhedrin had ordered that if anyone should know of Jesus' whereabouts, he was to report it to them. They were expecting trouble and wanted to prevent it by arresting Jesus on sight.

Since the Passover commemorated the deliverance of Israel from bondage, there was always at this feast the expectation that God would once again grant to His people a mighty deliverance. This hope centered in their concept of a political Messiah. Thus in the light of the belief of many that Jesus was the Christ. there was an unusual note of expectancy this particular year. Revolution was in the air. It was in order to protect their "place" and "nation" that the Sanhedrin had placed Jerusalem on the alert at this time.

1. *Six Days Before the Passover* (12:1, 9-11). This would be Friday before Passion Week. Perhaps late Friday afternoon Jesus

arrived in Bethany. And while it is not so stated, in all likelihood He stopped at the home of Lazarus and his sisters.

Word soon spread that He was there. Many people, therefore, came to the home (v. 9). This group probably was composed of both friendly Jews from Jerusalem and its environs and of pilgrims from other areas who had come to the feast. They not only wanted to see Jesus, but Lazarus, whom Jesus had raised from the dead. So widespread was news of this event that the chief priests had determined to put Lazarus to death also. His very presence was causing many to believe on Jesus.

At this point we face a problem in chronology. John relates the supper in the home of Simon the leper as though it happened on Friday evening (12:2-8). But Mark, followed by Matthew, places it on Tuesday evening. It seems wise to follow Mark's chronology. John probably related this event as he did, since it is his last mention of Bethany. So for the sake of continuity, we shall place it in its natural position as it is found in Mark.

2. *The Royal Entry* (12:12-19). This event occurred on Sunday morning following Jesus' arrival in Bethany on Friday. The synoptic gospels relate it in much greater detail. But John takes note of it as one of the major events which led up to the crucifixion the following Friday.

This entry into Jerusalem is usually called Jesus' "Triumphal Entry." But it has none of the earmarks of such events in the ancient world. When a king or a general returned victoriously to his capital city, he was given a triumphal entry in celebration of his victory. Usually he rode in his chariot or on a white horse, symbolizing victory, followed by defeated kings or other captives in chains. In this sense we may regard Ephesians 4:8 as Jesus' triumphal entry back into heaven.

But in His entry into Jerusalem Jesus came into His *capital city* as a king of peace, riding upon an ass. Therefore, we may more aptly call this His "Royal Entry." But it did have a very definite significance. Heretofore, Jesus had entered Jerusalem quietly and without fanfare. But here by a deliberate design (as seen in the synoptic gospels) He entered the city as a King of peace. In a manner not to be misunderstood, He challenged Jerusalem and her Jewish rulers either to receive or reject Him as the Christ, who was their Peace.

Actually the procession which accompanied Him on His royal entry was composed of two groups. It began with one group following Jesus as He rode down the western slopes of the Mount of Olives. This group cried, "Hosanna: Blessed is the King of

Israel that cometh in the name of the Lord" (v. 13). This was a Messianic cry, showing that they recognized Jesus as the Christ, the King of Israel. Another group of people came out of the city to meet this procession (v. 17). And converging, they escorted Jesus into Jerusalem.

All the while a group of helpless Pharisees watched the procession. They had failed in their purpose to arrest Jesus quietly. Now, "behold, the world is gone after him" (v. 19). They could only blame each other for their failure.

3. *The Visit of Certain Greeks* (12:20-33). This visit took place on Monday. Among those who came to the Passover were certain Greeks, probably Jewish proselytes. They had heard about Jesus. And learning that He was in Jerusalem, they sought an audience with Him. Apparently a group of people had gathered about Him to hear His teachings. So these Greeks, coming upon the crowd, may have recognized Philip, one of the Twelve. He was a Jew with a Greek name. Perhaps they had known him in Bethsaida of Galilee, which was his home. At any rate they said to him, "Sir, we would see Jesus" (v. 21). Philip told Andrew of their request, and together they relayed it to Jesus.

This request greatly affected Him. It appears that in their coming Jesus recognized the beginning of that innumerable host of Gentiles who would eventually believe in Him. But the cross must come before they could do so with understanding. Therefore, Jesus said, "The hour is come, that the Son of man should be glorified" (v. 23). The "hour" which He had foreseen from the beginning had arrived. Using the figure of a grain of wheat Jesus declared the necessity of His death. Unless a grain of wheat falls to the ground and dies to itself, it abides alone. It merely remains one grain of wheat. "But if it die, it bringeth forth much fruit" (v. 24). This is a principle of life. Any man who loves his natural life shall lose it, insofar as its true purpose is concerned. But if one would live eternally, he must choose to reject that life in the interest of the greater life, or that of his soul.

Jesus then made a statement which has proved to be a puzzle to interpreters. "Now is my soul troubled; and what shall I say? Father, save me from this hour: but for this cause came I unto this hour. Father, glorify thy name" (vv. 27, 28).

After anticipating "this hour" for so long, did Jesus now pray to be saved from it? This would seem to be the case, if we allow the punctuation to stand as it is in the King James Version. If Jesus did this, then it is strange indeed. Some endeavor to escape this position by interpreting Jesus' meaning as being not to escape the cross, but to be brought safely through it. But He had previously avowed His Resurrection from the dead. Therefore, why should He now pray for it?

The question hinges on whether Jesus actually was praying, or was He engaged in a soliloquy? If it was the latter, then this should be a question. And one Greek manuscript so punctuates it. Marcus Dods holds that it is a question. The author is inclined to agree with him. And if we read it as such, it reflects the constant attitude of Jesus toward the cross. Thus He said, "What shall I say? Father, save me from this hour? [Shall I say that?] But for this cause came I unto this hour. Father, glorify thy name." In this light Jesus, knowing that His hour had come, surrendered Himself to do His Father's will.

No sooner had He done this than a voice [*phonē*] came from heaven, saying, "I have both glorified it, and will glorify it again" (v. 28). Some who heard the sound *(phonē)* said that it thundered. Others thought that it was the voice of an angel speaking to Jesus. But Jesus said that it was truly a voice *(phonē)* which was given for their sakes, not His (v. 30). This within itself would indicate that Jesus did not pray to be delivered from the ordeal of the cross.

Then Jesus added that the next few days would be a judgment which would test the world. The prince of this world will be cast out. In His death and Resurrection the power of Satan will be broken (v. 31). "And I, if I be lifted up from the earth, will draw all men unto me," said Jesus (v. 32). John notes that in these words He signified the manner of His death. He might also have added that He told what would be the result of it.

4. *A Question and an Answer* (12:34-36). The crowd also understood Jesus as speaking of His death. So they raised a question. They had heard out of the law that Christ abides forever. How, then, could Jesus say that the Son of man must be lifted up or crucified? Was He speaking of someone else? And, if so, "who is this Son of man?" (v. 34)

Jesus replied by saying that for a little while the light is with them. While they have opportunity they should believe in the light, in order that they might be children of light instead of children of darkness. And with this He departed and hid Himself from them (v. 36).

5. *John's Commentary Upon Jesus' Words* (12:37-43). With reference to Jesus' challenge for the people to believe on Him, John notes that despite the fact that He had done many "signs"

before them still they did not believe on Him. This was in fulfill-ment of prophecy (v. 38; Isaiah 53:1; v. 40; Isaiah 6:10). Never-theless some did believe, and truly so, among them being certain members of the Sanhedrin. These certainly included Nicodemus and Joseph of Arimathea. Beyond this it is impossible to identify others. But even these did not confess Him openly. They feared the Pharisees, lest they should be put out of the synagogue (v. 42). And John adds sadly that they loved the praise of men more than they loved the praise of God (v. 43).

6. *John's Conclusion of Jesus' Public Ministry* (12:44-50). Whether or not these words of Jesus were spoken in this sequence is not clear. Since John notes in verse 36 that Jesus left, "and did hide himself from them," it appears that after this Jesus did not speak to the people any more. In that light verses 44-50 prob-ably represent the remainder of Jesus' statement which began in verse 36. John probably reports them as he does in order to form a fitting conclusion to Jesus' public ministry. (We know from the synoptic gospels that Jesus spent all of the next day debating with various groups of His enemies, and in teaching His disciples on the Mount of Olives.)

In a very real sense these words of Jesus might well be con-sidered as a summary of all that He had taught throughout His ministry. And it is understandable that He would sum up His message in a final appeal to the people of Jerusalem. Faith in Him was in truth faith in the Father. He came as light to the world (cf. vv. 35, 36), in order that those who believed in Him should not walk in darkness. Those who rejected Him would surely come to judgment. He did not come for the purpose of judgment, but "to save the world" (v. 47). But by the very nature of the case those who rejected His words would be judged by them. They will be the basis of judgment at the last day.

This is because Jesus has not spoken by His own authority alone. "But the Father which sent me, he gave me a commandment, what I should say, and what I should speak" (v. 49). The form of the verb "gave" means that this is an abiding commission. He is God's complete, final revelation to man.

Jesus added that He knows in His soul that God's command-ment is life eternal. He alone has the words of eternal life (6:68). And man's reaction to His words determines his eternal destiny. Then Jesus concluded with words which have in them the ring of finality. "Whatsoever I speak therefore, even as the Father said unto me, so I speak" (v. 50). It is a fitting finale to His pub-lic ministry.

7. *A Supper in Bethany* (12:2-8). The synoptic gospels give a rather full account of events on Tuesday, the "day of controversy." The Sadducees, Pharisees, and Herodians combined their forces in a vain effort to discredit Jesus with the people. At times the verbal conflict was sharp indeed. It concluded with Jesus thoroughly condemning the Pharisees in the most excoriating words which ever fell from His lips (Matthew 23). It was divine wrath falling upon those who definitely and finally had rejected divine love. With this Jesus left the temple never to return. There was poetic justice in this act. For in essence it was God deserting the temple. Henceforth He would dwell in the hearts of believers (I Corinthians 6:19).

On His way back to Bethany Jesus and the Twelve stopped to rest on their way up the Mount of Olives. There Jesus taught them with respect to the coming destruction of Jerusalem (A.D. 70), the sign of His Second Coming, and of the end of the age (Matthew 24, 25).

That evening (Tuesday) Jesus and His disciples, along with Lazarus, were guests at dinner in the home of Simon the leper. Matthew and Mark, in addition to John, record this event. The first two give the basic facts in the case.

While they were eating a woman came with an alabaster cruse of spikenard, a very costly ointment. It was a gift fit for a king. In typical oriental fashion the woman broke the cruse, and poured its contents upon Jesus' head (Matthew and Mark) and feet (John). It was an expression of the highest love which did not count the cost of its expression.

However, the disciples failed to appreciate this act. They were filled with indignation. "To what purpose hath this waste of the ointment been made?" they asked (Mark 14:4). And then they added that it might have been sold for above three hundred *denarii*, or for more than $51.00, and given to the poor.

Jesus, on the other hand, understood and appreciated the woman's act. Therefore, He told them to stop troubling her, for she had wrought a good work upon Him. The poor they had with them always, but He would not be with them always. Then He interpreted the meaning of her act. She had anointed Him for His burial. He knew that His death was at hand.

The disciples might resent the woman's act. But history would not do so. For "wheresoever this gospel shall be preached in the whole world, there shall also this, that this woman hath done, be told for a memorial of her" (Matthew 26:13).

John tells substantially the same story. But he does so with a purpose. Nowhere else is his purpose to supplement the synoptic gospels more clearly seen. A comparative reading of the three accounts makes this purpose quite evident (Matthew 26:6-13; Mark 14:3-9; John 12:2-8).

In the synoptic accounts the only person mentioned by name is the host. But John adds the names of the principal characters, without which the account is incomplete. The earlier writers probably omitted their names for a good reason. At the time when they wrote, these people, except Judas, may have been alive. And to mention them by name could have endangered their lives. But John who wrote much later, probably after they had died, used their names in order to clarify the record.

For instance, he adds that Lazarus was present and that Martha served. Some have supposed from this that she was the wife of Simon the leper. But there is no real basis for such a supposition. It is more reasonable to note that she was merely a neighbor who came in to help out. This is in keeping with her nature as noted in Luke 10:40.

But one of the most striking additions is that John names the woman who anointed Jesus. It was Mary of Bethany. And again she was acting in accord with her nature as pointed out by Luke. But the interesting thing is that, whereas both Matthew and Mark speak of a memorial unto this woman, neither mentions her name. Except for John this would have remained an anonymous memorial.

Another notable addition is that John names Judas Iscariot as the one who criticized Mary for her deed of love. In all likelihood he began the criticism, and the other disciples joined in. And John adds the further note that Judas had no concern for the poor. He kept the "bag" of Jesus' little band, and had been stealing from it. He wanted the money for himself.

The part which Judas played in this episode also explains Matthew 26:14-16 and Mark 14:10, 11. For Judas went directly from this supper to bargain with the chief priests concerning his deed of betrayal. He was stung into action by Jesus' rebuke. The Lord's explanation of Mary's act as anointing Him for burial could mean but one thing. Jesus was going to die. Judas had failed to get his hands on the $51.00. So he decided to get what he could out of the debacle, as it seemed to him to be. In so doing he settled for less than half the amount. For the thirty pieces of silver would be worth about twenty-five dollars.

8. *A Study in Contrasts* (12:3, 4). One can hardly escape the fact that John's account of this supper was intended, among other

things, to present a contrast between Mary and Judas. "Then Mary . . . but Judas . . . which should betray him." It is likely that they were the first two people who fully realized that Jesus was going to die. And in that realization the true nature of each came to light.

Both had enjoyed an intimate fellowship with Jesus. They had heard His teachings and had known His love. Yet in the crisis they reacted so differently.

We know from Mary's deed of love that she somehow knew that Jesus' death was near. There was nothing which she might do to prevent it. What, then, could she do? She could show Him that she loved Him, and insofar as she was able she entered into His experience. Therefore, she asked herself a question, "What can I do for Jesus?" And she anointed Him for burial.

Judas, on the other hand, also realized that Jesus was going to die. He had never been a true disciple of His. He envisioned an earthly kingdom in which he might occupy a prominent place. But more and more he had come to realize that he was mistaken. This thought had probably taken root in his mind following the feeding of the five thousand, when Jesus had thrust aside the abortive effort to make Him king. Jesus' Royal Entry had failed to bring forth a royal proclamation as Judas saw it. Now Jerusalem was filled with rumors about the Sanhedrin's resolve to put Jesus to death. To Judas it was only a matter of time until they would accomplish their purpose.

Yes, Jesus was going to die. Judas had done all that he knew to do in an effort to force Jesus' hand in setting up His kingdom. But he had concluded that Jesus was no king, only a speaker of fine words or an idle dreamer. So if Jesus were going to die, he might just as well try to salvage something from the failure of his elusive dream. Thus Judas also asked himself a question, "What can Jesus do for me?" And he bargained to betray Him for thirty pieces of silver, the price of a slave.

Therefore, on this Tuesday night before the crucifixion both Mary and Judas achieved a memorial. Mary's is a memorial of love and unselfishness. Judas' is a memorial of hate and greed. Mary's ointment not only perfumed the supper chamber in Simon's home. The winds of time have wafted it throughout the world, as an odor of a sweet ointment of utter devotion to the Son of God.

But Judas, ah, Judas! What is his memorial? The chief priests took his ill-gotten gain, and with it bought a potter's field in which to bury, not Jews, but foreigners (Matthew 27:7). And they did not even name it "Judas Memorial Cemetery"! He grabbed for everything and got nothing. People name their boys after Paul, and their dogs after Nero. But the only thing that is named after Judas is the goat which leads sheep to the slaughter.

He inherited a noble name, Judas, or Judah. But what a legacy he passed on! He will forever be known as "Judas Iscariot, Simon's son, which should betray him" (v. 4).

FOR FURTHER STUDY

1. For a full account of Jesus' Royal Entry into Jerusalem read Matthew 21:1-11, 14-17; Mark 11:1-11; Luke 19:29-44. What was the purpose of this event?
2. Were Jesus' words in John 12:17, 28a a prayer or a soliloquy? Read J. B. Phillips' translation of these verses in *The New Testament in Modern English*.
3. In what way was Jesus' crucifixion and Resurrection a judgment or crisis of the world? In what manner were these events a casting out of Satan, the prince of this world?
4. Compare John 12:2-8 with Matthew 26:6-13 and Mark 14:3-9, noting the supplementary details added by John.
5. Read Matthew 26:14-16; Mark 14:10, 11; Luke 22:3-6 noting the relationship between the supper in Bethany and the betrayal by Judas.
6. In the light of the contrast between Mary of Bethany and Judas, where do you stand in your attitude toward Jesus?

CHAPTER 9

The Foreboding Shadows

(John 13-17)

The gospels do not record what Jesus did on Wednesday of Passion Week. He probably spent the day resting and teaching His disciples. From the synoptic record we learn that about noon on Thursday He sent Peter and John to prepare for the Passover meal which was to be eaten in a home selected by Jesus. The Passover feast began at sunset on the 15th Nisan. During the afternoon of 14th Nisan these disciples secured the passover lamb at the temple, and had it slain by the priests. Then they roasted it, and along with other victuals prepared the meal. Shortly before sunset Jesus and the other disciples arrived for the meal. It was served probably in the guest room, the "upper room," of the home.

It was a time of great stress for Jesus. Knowing that the end was near His heart went out in love to the disciples (v. 1). His heart was heavy because of the treachery of Judas. And we know from Luke 22:24 that His burden was increased by the disciples as they contended for the chief reclining places about the table.

1. *Jesus' Lesson in Humility* (13:4-17). During the meal Jesus rose from the table, girded Himself with a towel, took a basin of water, and began to wash the disciples' feet. It was

customary for the host to have a slave who rinsed the dust from
the feet of his arriving guests. Having no such slave, Jesus performed this task Himself. But when He came to Peter, that disciple
protested that Jesus should not render so menial a service for him.
And there followed a dialogue which is largely lost in the translation.

Peter said, "Thou shalt never *rinse* my feet." Jesus replied,
"If I *rinse* thee not, thou hast no part with me" (v. 8). In typical
fashion Peter replied that if this were the case, "Lord, not my feet
only, but also my hands and my head" (v. 9). There must have
been a twinkle in Jesus' eyes as He said, "He that is *bathed* needeth
not save to *rinse* his feet, but is clean every whit" (v. 10, author's
italics). In short, if Peter took a bath before coming, he needed
only to have the dust rinsed from his feet. Then Jesus added in
a mystical note that they were spiritually clean, all save one. For
He knew the heart of Judas.

Having completed the act, Jesus applied the lesson. If He,
their Lord and Master, had performed this menial service for them
they should do the same for one another. True greatness lies not in
outward honor, but in humble service (v. 16). Feet washing is not
an ordinance commanded by Jesus. It was an "example" (v. 15)
in humility. And if His followers would practice it, they would
be happy (blessed) in the doing of it (v. 17).

2. *Jesus Points Out the Betrayer* (13:18-30). For the first
time He pointed out clearly that one of His own little band would
betray Him. "He that eateth bread with me hath lifted up his
heel against me" (v. 18). This did not identify the person, but it
indicated the intimacy which should be betrayed. And then He
said that "one of you shall betray me" (v. 21). The disciples
cast wondering glances at one another. One of the disciples "whom
Jesus loved," probably John himself, was leaning on Jesus' bosom,
the place of highest honor. Peter asked him to get Jesus to point
out the betrayer. So in reply to John's question, "Lord, who is it?"
Jesus said that it was the one to whom He should give the sop.
They were all dipping out of a common dish of gravy. It was customary for the host to honor a guest by giving him a morsel of
dipped bread. So Jesus gave it to Judas. Therefore, this did not
tell Peter what he wanted to know. But John knew. And so did
Judas.

When Jesus gave Judas the sop, He told him to do quickly
what he planned to do. It was a custom to give food to the poor
during the Passover. So hearing Jesus' words, the others thought
that Jesus was sending Judas, who carried the "bag," to buy pro-

visions for that purpose. But Judas knew otherwise. Therefore, he left the room immediately to go on his evil errand.

John notes that "it was night" (v. 30). Since it was the time of the full moon, this could not refer to physical darkness. It was John's way of saying that Judas went fully into the darkness of evil. Jesus is Light. To come to Him is to come into the light. To go from Him is to go into darkness. So Judas went out into the "night."

John does not record the instituting of the Lord's Supper, since it had been done by the synoptic writers. But a comparison of his account with theirs indicates that this was done after Judas had left the room. The Memorial Supper was and is for baptized *believers* only. Most likely Judas had been baptized. But he was not a *believer*.

3. *The Son of Man Glorified* (13:31-38). Judas' departure meant that the cross drew ever nearer. Jesus would soon be "glorified." Thus He would go where the disciples cannot follow (v. 33). And because of this it was all the more necessary that they should love one another. It would be by this that all men would know that they were His disciples (v. 35).

When Peter heard Jesus say that they could not follow Him, he knew that He spoke of danger. So he vowed that while the others might not do so, in order to follow Jesus he was ready to die in the process. But Jesus knew Peter better than he knew himself. So He told him that "the cock shall not crow [in the morning], till thou hast denied me thrice" (v. 38).

4. *Jesus' Words of Comfort* (14:1-31). Gloom settled over the disciples. They now realized fully that Jesus was going to die. And they would be left alone. But Jesus spoke words of comfort to them, words that have been the pillow for broken hearts down through the ages.

Do we need to quote them? "Let not your heart be troubled . . . ." (v. 1). Each of you can continue them from blessed memory. What was Jesus' secret for an untroubled heart? Faith in God and in Him. He was going away, but He would return to receive them into the place which He was going to prepare for them. "That where I am, there ye may be also" (v. 3). Jesus reminded them that they knew where He was going, and they knew the way. When Thomas showed his ignorance of all this, Jesus said, "I am the way, the truth, and the life: no man cometh unto the Father, but by me" (v. 6). He added that if they knew Him, they should know the Father also. Philip added his request that Jesus would show them the Father, and that would be sufficient. But Jesus

reminded him of His many teachings about His oneness with the
Father (vv. 9-11). If they would not believe His words, at least
they should believe His works (v. 11). Furthermore, if they
believed in Him, they would do even greater works than He had
done. Not greater in degree but in scope. This was because He
was returning to the Father. If they would pray "in my name,"
He promised that He would do it, "that the Father may be glorified
in the Son" (vv. 13, 14).

This thought of greater works and prayer led Jesus to give
the promise of the Holy Spirit. Note that they were not to pray
for the coming of the Spirit. "And I will pray the Father, and he
will give you another Comforter, that he may abide with you for
ever" (v. 16). Jesus is going away, but they shall know His abiding presence through the Spirit.

The word "Comforter" renders the word *Paraclete,* the one
being called alongside. A *paraclete* was a lawyer, especially one for
the defense. He is to be the Advocate (cf. I John 2:1) of God before
their hearts. This word might also be translated as "encourager,"
hence the Comforter. And note that He is to be "another" Comforter. This means another of the same kind, like Jesus. Marcus
Dods called the Holy Spirit "Jesus' *alter ego*" or "other self," and
B. H. Carroll called Him "the other Jesus." What Jesus had been
to them, and more, the Holy Spirit would be to them. Jesus had
been *with* them. The Holy Spirit "shall be in you" (v. 17).

The disciples felt that they were being left alone. But Jesus
said, "I will not leave you comfortless [orphans]: I will come to
you" (v. 18). For a little while they will not see Him. But after
His Resurrection they will see Him. And because He lives, they
will know life in Him. Even after His Resurrection they will know
His presence, and that of the Father, through the indwelling
Spirit (vv. 20-23).

These things Jesus had spoken to the disciples while He was
with them. But when the Holy Spirit comes, He will teach them
all things. Furthermore, He will bring to their remembrance all
that Jesus has said to them (v. 26).

And then He gave to them His legacy of peace (v. 27). It
is not the peace of the world which is conditioned by circum-
stances. It is His abiding peace. Therefore, they should not
trouble their hearts or be afraid. They were sad because He was
going away. But if they really love Him, they will rejoice, because
He is returning to His Father. He had told them these things
to prepare them beforehand for the ordeal which awaits them.

Now when they come to pass, they will have an additional reason to believe in Him.

From this time on Jesus would not talk much with them. "For the prince of this world cometh, and hath nothing in me" (v. 30). Jesus was going forth to accomplish the will of His Father. And this would be the supreme expression of His love for the Father.

With these words Jesus said, "Arise, let us go hence" (v. 31). So they left the sanctuary of the upper room, to go toward Jesus' rendezvous with destiny. There still remained the agony of Gethsemane before that of the cross.

5. *Jesus' Challenge to Service* (15:1-27). Jesus continued to teach His disciples as they walked through the streets of Jerusalem toward Gethsemane. The subject dealt with the condition under which they were to render fruitful service to God and their obligation to do so in the unfolding future. The condition was that they should abide in Him. The obligation rested upon the fact that they had been chosen to serve.

Jesus likened Himself to "the true vine" with His Father as the husbandman (v. 1). The disciples were the branches which grew out of the vine. Only as the branches abide in the Vine can they bear fruit. "For," said Jesus, "apart from me ye can do nothing" (v. 5). Fruitless branches will be pruned away in order that the Vine may bear more fruit (v. 2). This should not be construed to mean a loss of salvation. The subject here is fruitbearing, not salvation. Jesus simply employed a well-known figure of speech to express the former truth. Failure to abide in Him would result in a wasted life (v. 6; cf. I Corinthians 3:9-15). It is vital, therefore, that the disciples should abide in Christ and in His love (vv. 7-11). Furthermore, they should love one another even as Christ loves them. "Greater love hath no man than this, that a man lay down his life for his friends" (v. 13). Jesus will do this for them, and they must be willing to do the same for each other.

In John 13:16 Jesus had spoken of the relationship between Him and the disciples as that of Lord and servant or slave. Now He calls them His friends. "Ye are my friends, if ye do whatsoever I command you" (v. 14). A slave does not know what his lord is doing. But as His friends, Jesus has made known to them the full revelation of the Father.

As His friends they have an obligation to bear fruit. He has chosen and appointed them for this very purpose (v. 16). And they are to keep on bearing fruit, knowing that in such service they have the assurance that whatsoever they shall ask in His name the Father will give to them.

In this service the disciples are to expect to experience the hatred of the world (vv. 18-25). It hates Jesus, and it will hate them. The world loves its own. But since they are not of the world, the world will persecute them as it has persecuted Jesus. The Christian Gospel is a judgment against the world's sin. It both reveals its sin and is God's witness against it. But when the Holy Spirit comes in power, He will bear witness of Jesus. And since the disciples have been with Him from the beginning they, in the Spirit's power, are to bear witness also (vv. 26, 27).

6. *Jesus' Words of Courage* (16:1-33). Jesus told them these things so that when persecution comes, they will not be caused to stumble thereby (16:1-4). Now He is going away, and they are sorrowful. But it is necessary that He depart in order that the Paraclete may come (vv. 7-11). He will be their ally in the spread of the Gospel. They are to bear witness. But He will convict the world of sin, righteousness, and judgment. It is in the Spirit's convicting power alone that their efforts shall bear fruit.

The disciples were not yet ready to hear all that Jesus wished to tell them. But the Holy Spirit would guide them into all truth (vv. 12-15). He would not speak of Himself but of Christ. He will declare to them "the coming things." And He will not glorify Himself, but Christ. This within itself is a good test as to whether or not a system of religion is of the Holy Spirit. Any theology which exalts the Holy Spirit above Jesus is not of the Holy Spirit. For "he shall glorify me," said Jesus (v. 14).

Then Jesus reminded them again that He was going away (vv. 16-31). When they saw Him on the cross, and dead, they would weep and lament. In that hour the world would rejoice, but it would be of short duration. On the other hand, the disciples' sorrow would soon give way to rejoicing when they saw Jesus after the Resurrection. And it would be a joy which no one could take from them. As a woman forgets the travail after the child is born, and rejoices, so would be their joy after the travail of His death which would make possible His Resurrection.

After a further reassurance concerning the efficacy of prayer, Jesus summed up the meaning of the Incarnation (v. 28). He came forth from the Father, and in His coming the Incarnation became a permanent fact. Even when He ascends back to the Father, the Incarnation will continue to be a reality. For in His resurrection body He will still bear the evidence of His redemptive work. In essence, Jesus said that He came from the Father, and would return to the Father. While on earth in the flesh, He was the same One who had been eternally with the Father. After His return to heaven He would be the same One who was on earth.

The disciples understood this plain teaching. Therefore, they avowed their faith that He had come forth from the Father. But Jesus asked, "Do ye now believe?" (v. 31). Their faith was genuine. But the hour was at hand when it would be tried. They would be scattered as sheep by the wolves. They would desert Jesus. But He would not be alone. For the Father would be with Him. These things Jesus had told them that they might have peace in the storm which was about to break about them. And then He reassured them (and us), not only for the hours ahead, but for all time to come. "In the world ye shall have tribulation: but be of good cheer [courage]; I have overcome the world" (v. 33). It is a complete and abiding victory, as seen in the perfect tense of the verb form rendered, "I have overcome."

7. *Jesus' High Priestly Prayer* (17:1-24). By this time Jesus and His little band probably had arrived at a spot just outside the temple area. Evidently He stopped and there prayed what might be called His High Priestly prayer. He was the great High Priest praying to God before the sacrifice was made. This prayer naturally divides itself into three parts as Jesus prayed for Himself, for His present disciples, and for all who henceforth should believe on Him.

First, Jesus prayed for Himself (vv. 1-8). "Father, the hour is come; glorify thy Son, that thy Son also may glorify thee." The Father had empowered Him to give eternal life to all whom the Father has given to Him. He defined eternal life as knowing by experience the only true God, and Jesus Christ, whom He had sent into the world (v. 3). Jesus has glorified the Father on earth, in that He has accomplished the work which was given to Him to do. Now He prayed that the Father, in turn, would return to Him His preincarnate glory.

Jesus avowed that He had manifested the Father's name to the disciples which were given to Him by the Father. And they have kept God's Word. They knew that all things pertaining to Jesus came from the Father. Furthermore, they knew that the Father had sent His Son into the world (v. 8).

Second, Jesus prayed for His present disciples (vv. 9-19). "I pray for them." He did not pray for the world but for these whom the Father had given to Him out of the world. Jesus was leaving them to return to His Father. So He prayed that the Father would keep them through His authority and power. He prayed, furthermore, that they might continue to be one in spirit, even as He and the Father were one. They were to be left as witnesses in a hostile world. So Jesus did not pray that they should be taken out of the world. Instead He prayed that they should be guarded from the evil one.

As the Father had sent Him into the world, He was sending His disciples into the world. Therefore, He prayed that God would "sanctify" them through His truth, even His Word. The word rendered "sanctify" basically means to dedicate or to set apart for God's service. A sanctified person should endeavor to live apart from sin. But sanctification does not mean sinless perfection. A sanctified person is a "saint." And in the New Testament all Christians are called "saints" (cf. II Corinthians 1:1).

That the word "sanctify" does not mean to get rid of sin is seen in verse 19. Jesus said, "And for their sakes I sanctify myself, that they also might be sanctified through thy truth." The meaning is that Jesus dedicated Himself to the cross for their sakes, to the end that they might be set apart to God's service through His truth.

Third, Jesus prayed for all who henceforth should believe on Him (vv. 20-26). He further prayed that all of these might be one, "as thou, Father, art in me, and I in thee, that they also may be one in us: that the world may believe that thou hast sent me." Again, as in verse 11, Jesus prayed for a oneness of spirit. He was not praying for outward organic union. The Father and the Son are distinct personalities within the Godhead. But in their relationship as one they enjoy the unity of spirit and love. It was this for which Jesus prayed with respect to His disciples.

Then Jesus prayed that all whom the Father had given to Him might be with Him in heaven. He longed for them to behold His glory which the Father had given Him. This glory was an expression of the Father's love before the foundation of the world. Note once again Jesus' claim to pre incarnate existence.

8. *Jesus' Summary of His Ministry* (17:25, 26). Now the prayer proper was ended. But as Jesus continued to commune with the Father, He summed up the total of His ministry during His sojourn on earth and in the unfolding future. In verse 11 He had addressed God as "Holy Father." Now He addressed Him as "O righteous Father." As in the former He appealed to God's holiness, in the latter He called on His righteousness.

Even after thirty-three years of His incarnate existence, the world has not known the Father. But Jesus has known Him. And through Him His disciples have known that the Father has sent Him into the world.

During His earthly ministry Jesus has made known the Father's name to His present disciples. And through the Holy Spirit He will continue to make it known to future generations. It will be to the end that the love with which the Father has loved the Son may be in them who believe in Him, and, furthermore, that He may be in them.

This was the purpose of the Incarnation. John began his gospel by declaring that the eternal God in Christ became flesh, in order that He might fully reveal God to men in terms of their own understanding. Step by step he has followed Jesus as He unfolded the meaning of God's love for a lost humanity. The world rejected that revelation. But some came out of the world to believe in Him whom the Father had sent. Now Jesus' public ministry to the world is finished. His private teaching of His little band of intimates is over.

But the greatest revelation of God's love is yet to come. And before the sun should set at the close of another day the world would know that "God commendeth his love toward us, in that, while we were yet sinners, Christ died for us" (Romans 5:8).

FOR FURTHER STUDY

1. Luke 22:24-30 probably comes just before John 13:1-20. To understand better the significance of the latter read the former and then the latter without stopping.
2. For an excellent devotional treatment of John 14-17 read Yates, *Preaching From John's Gospel*, Broadman, 1964, pp. 126-151.
3. Jesus called the Holy Spirit "another-of-the-same-kind of Comforter" (John 14:16). In what ways is the Holy Spirit like Jesus in His ministry to and through the Christian?
4. If the fruit of a grape vine is grapes, what is the fruit of a Christian life?
5. How may the Christian abide in Christ?
6. List some ways that the Holy Spirit makes us fruitful Christians.
7. What does it mean to pray "in Jesus' name"?

CHAPTER 10

The Arrest, Trial, Crucifixion, And Resurrection

(John 18-21)

When Jesus had finished His prayer, He led His disciples out of Jerusalem through the eastern gate. Descending from the city they crossed the brook Kidron. This means "the brook of Cedars." Just beyond the brook was a garden called Gethsemane. It was a place to which Jesus often had gone to pray (vv. 1, 2). Probably shortly after midnight, Friday morning, He and the disciples entered the garden. Tourists are still shown such a garden, even to the "Rock of Agony" on which tradition says that Jesus prayed. Whether or not this is the true garden, it must have been somewhere near.

John does not record the prayer experience of Jesus in Gethsemane. But by relating the visit to the garden, He recognizes the accounts found in the other gospels. It was in this garden that Judas betrayed Jesus.

1. *The Betrayal of Jesus* (18:3-11). After Judas had secured a band of temple police and Roman soldiers, he probably returned to the upper room. Failing to find Jesus there he surmised that He had gone to Gethsemane to pray. So he led the arresting detail there. By the time they arrived Jesus had finished His prayer

vigil. Therefore, He greeted them with the question, "Whom seek ye?" (v. 4). They said, "Jesus of Nazareth." And Jesus answered, "I am he" (v. 5). John does not record the kiss of betrayal by Judas. He simply mentions his presence.

Evidently this armed band was awed, even afraid, in Jesus' presence. They knew of His supernatural power. So when He identified Himself to them they stepped backward so quickly that they tripped and fell to the ground (v. 6). Then after a second identification of Himself, Jesus said, "If therefore ye seek me, let these [the disciples] go their way" (v. 8). He did not want to endanger them because of what was happening to Him.

When Peter saw the officers move forward to take Jesus, he pulled out his sword and cut off the right ear of Malchus, a servant of the high priest (v. 10). He was aiming at Malchus' head, but the man must have dodged expertly. Peter was true to his word as being willing to die for Jesus. Why did he do this? A careful reading of Luke 22:36-38 reveals that Jesus had told the disciples to secure swords before they left the upper room. They found two which probably belonged to the owner of the house. Why these swords? They were to be used to guard Jesus until He was ready to be taken. He would die but it would be on a cross, and that when He was ready. He must win the victory in Gethsemane before going to Calvary. The two swords and the fact that Jesus divided the disciples into two groups in the garden, one just inside and the other further in the garden, are suggestive. Did each group have one sword? Certainly Peter of the inner group had one.

So when Peter pulled his sword, he thought that he was doing what he had been told. But Jesus was now ready to be taken. So He told Peter to put up his sword. And thereby He probably saved his life. Jesus was now ready to drink the "cup" which the Father had given to Him. He no longer needed protection from His enemies.

2. *The Arrest of Jesus* (18:12). "Then the band and the captain and officers of the Jews took Jesus, and bound him." It was quite an anticlimax for them. They had come armed for battle. But Jesus surrendered without a struggle. No man took His life from Him. He laid it down of Himself.

3. *The Trial of Jesus* (18:13 - 19:16). The trial of Jesus consisted of two phases, the Jewish and the Roman. And in the full account of all four gospels each of these contained three stages. The Jewish: before Annas; before the Sanhedrin prior to dawn;

before the Sanhedrin after dawn. The Roman: before Pilate; before Herod Antipas; before Pilate a second time. But John condenses His account into two Jewish phases and one Roman (even though his record blends with that of the synoptic gospels). And since the former was more of an empty gesture, John concentrates on the latter.

From Gethsemane Jesus was taken first before Annas, Caiaphas' father-in-law (v. 13). As a former high priest he was still quite a power among both the Jews and the Romans. Since Judas' betrayal had caught the Sanhedrin unprepared, they probably wanted Annas to hold a preliminary hearing in order to get some charge to bring against Jesus. A charge brought by Annas would carry weight, especially with the Romans.

Annas asked Jesus about His disciples and His teaching (v. 19). Jesus ignored the inquiry about His disciples. As for His teaching, He had taught openly in the synagogues and the temple. His teachings were no secret. So why ask Him about them? Why not ask those who had heard Him (vv. 20, 21)?

An officer slapped Jesus for what he took to be an impudent reply to Annas. To this brutal attack Jesus replied that if He had spoken evil, let the officer prove it. Otherwise, why did he strike Him? But it was evident to Annas that he would get nothing out of Jesus, so he sent Him on to Caiaphas (v. 24).

This would be the first appearance before the Sanhedrin prior to dawn. We know from the synoptic gospels that after false witnesses failed to convict Jesus, Caiaphas put Him on oath. And under oath He admitted that He was the Christ, the Son of God. Therefore, the Sanhedrin voted unanimously that He had blasphemed and was worthy of death. Under Jewish law a unanimous verdict was supposed to be equal to an acquittal. But not so with Jesus.

Then after dawn the Sanhedrin met again, formally to vote Jesus to be guilty of death. And they led Him away to Pilate (v. 28).

In the meantime, something had been happening outside in the court of Caiaphas' house (vv. 15-18, 25-27). Peter and another disciple (John?) had followed the group from Gethsemane to Caiaphas' house. During the course of Jesus' Jewish trial on three different occasions Peter had been asked about his relationship to Jesus. And each time he had denied being a disciple of Jesus. With the third denial, he heard a cock crow. Jesus' prophecy about him had been fulfilled.

While the Sanhedrin was permitted to govern the Jews in civil and religious matters, the Romans reserved to themselves the right to inflict capital punishment. So even though the Jewish court had adjudged Jesus as being worthy of death, He had to be taken before Pilate for sentence and execution.

Pilate was the procurator of Judea (A.D. 26-36), ruling under the Roman propraetor of the province of Syria. He despised the Jews. His record in dealing with them was far from being a good one. He showed no regard whatever for their religious traditions, a fact which more than once resulted in their violent opposition. On one occasion he had even taken money from the sacred treasure of the temple with which to build an aqueduct into Jerusalem. Even though his purpose was to improve the water supply of the city, the Jews strongly resented his taking the treasury money to finance it. And it was public information that Pilate was not above receiving bribes for some desired favor. It is little wonder then that the Roman trial of Jesus reflects the antagonism which existed between Pilate and the Jewish rulers.

Pilate ordinarily lived in Caesarea on the Mediterranean coast. He came to Jerusalem only when his official duties required it. One such occasion was the Passover. Because nationalistic feelings ran high at that time, he always brought military reinforcements to preserve the peace. When he came to Jerusalem he stayed in the palace which had been built by Herod the Great. Since it was early in the morning probably it was to this palace that the Jewish rulers brought Jesus.

The Jews refused to be defiled by entering the residence of a Gentile (v. 28). So Pilate came out to them. In reply to his question as to their charge against Jesus, they said contemptuously, "If he were not a malefactor, we would not have delivered him unto thee" (v. 30). Figuring that it involved some religious question, Pilate told them to handle the matter. But they quickly reminded him that they had no authority to put a man to death. They had already condemned Jesus, regardless of what Pilate might decide.

Pilate took Jesus inside the judgment hall to question Him. "Art thou the king of the Jews?" he asked. Jesus, in turn, asked if he said this of himself, or did someone else tell him. Scornfully Pilate asked, "Am I a Jew? Thine own nation and the chief priests have delivered thee unto me: what hast thou done?" (v. 35). Jesus commented that His kingdom was not of this world, else His servants would fight to defend Him. He, therefore, admitted to having a kingdom, but not an earthly one.

Pilate ignored this point as he asked further, "Art thou a king then?" (v. 37) His question invited an affirmative answer. So, in effect, Jesus admitted that He was when He said, "Thou sayest that I am a king" (v. 37). In other words, Pilate himself had said so. But Jesus added that His was a kingdom of truth. The governor showed his unconcern and ignorance when with contempt he asked, "What is truth?" (v. 38)

Pilate saw that Jesus was guilty of no crime against Rome, or one worthy of death. And going out to the Jews he told them so. From the synoptic gospels we know that at this point the Jews countered by saying that according to their law He should die. For from Galilee to Jerusalem Jesus had stirred up the people, presumably inciting to revolution, which was a false charge, of course. When Pilate heard the word "Galilee," he saw an out. So he sent Jesus to Herod Antipas, the tetrarch of Galilee, who was in Jerusalem at the time. But he soon returned Him to Pilate.

John takes up the story again at this point. Pilate reminded the Jews of a custom whereby on occasion Rome, to placate the Jews, would release from prison some prisoner of their choice. So he proposed to release Jesus. The synoptics record that he gave the Jews a choice between Jesus and Barabbas, a noted revolutionary and murderer. To Pilate's surprise they chose Barabbas (v. 40).

Still trying to get out of his predicament Pilate ordered Jesus scourged (19:1). Since he had pronounced Him innocent, this cruel beating was illegal. The soldiers then made a crown out of thorns and put it on Jesus' head. Throwing a purple robe about Him, they mocked Him and slapped Him. Then Pilate led Him out for the crowd to see. He reaffirmed Jesus' innocence, and cried, "Behold the man!" (v. 5) Perhaps Jesus' appearance in such fashion would incite pity, and also show how ridiculous was the charge of treason against so pitiable a figure. But the Jewish rulers cried, "Crucify him" (v. 6). The weakling Pilate replied, "Take ye him, and crucify him: for I find no fault in him" (v. 6). This was the prided Roman justice at its worst!

The Jews did not take Pilate's bait. Instead, they reminded him that according to their law Jesus should die, since He had "made himself the [a] Son of God" (v. 7). They now admitted their real reason for wanting Jesus to be crucified.

This frightened the superstitious Roman all the more. So he took Jesus inside again to question Him. But He remained silent. When Pilate reminded Him that he had the power either to crucify or to release Him, Jesus said that he had no power except that which was given to him from above. So Pilate "kept on seeking" to release Jesus (v. 12). But the Jews cried out that if he did so, he was not Caesar's friend. This was an implied threat to report Pilate's evil deeds to Caesar.

Even so, he made a final effort to release Jesus. He brought Him outside again, saying, "Behold your King!" (v. 14) The Jews cried again for His crucifixion, avowing that they had no king but Caesar. So Pilate surrendered. He turned Jesus over to the detail of soldiers who were to carry out the sentence. And they led Him away.

4. *The Crucifixion of Jesus* (19:17-37). It is impossible to locate accurately Golgotha or Calvary. Tradition says that it was the site on which stands the Church of the Holy Sepulchre. But many questions have been raised about this. The place was outside the city wall (Hebrews 13:12). To date it has not been shown that this location was outside any of the walls of Jerusalem. Gordon's Calvary, which is outside the walls, has been suggested as the place. And there is much to be said in its favor. Perhaps we shall never know the true site. Possibly God does not intend that we shall know.

But wherever it was, there "they crucified him" between two thieves (v. 18). And it took place on "the preparation," which was a technical term for Friday (v. 14). According to custom the upright piece of the cross stood in a hole in the ground. The cross piece was placed flat on the ground. Jesus, stark naked, was made to lie down with His arms outstretched along the cross piece. To render Him helpless His arms and legs were jerked out of joint. After His hands had been nailed to the crossbeam, His body was drawn up into position. Then Jesus' feet were crossed, and, with a spike, nailed to the cross. There He was suspended, about two feet above the ground.

In keeping with Roman law a title board was placed above Jesus' head. That all might see, the *crime* for which He died was written thereon. It read JESUS OF NAZARETH THE KING OF THE JEWS (v. 19). So Jesus died as a King.

John notes that this was a tri-lingual sign: Hebrew (Aramaic), Greek, and Latin. Perhaps Pilate used the first two since everyone could read one or the other. Latin was the official language of the Empire. Since John alone mentions the three languages, we are tempted to look behind this fact for a mystical meaning as well as the practical one. These languages represented the three great streams of life in that day: religion, culture, and government or law. And they converged in nailing the Son of God to a cross. Hebrew religion rejected Him. Greek culture ignored Him. Roman law crucified Him. Therefore, the guilt for Jesus' death rests upon all men, and in every age.

When the chief priests saw this "title" they went to Pilate with a protest. Said they, "Write not, The King of the Jews; but that he said, I am the King of the Jews" (v. 21). But the Roman governor finally got up enough courage to stand his ground. He said, "What I have written I have written" (v. 22). Literally, "What I have written stands written." So the charge remained for all time. And technically he was right. For this was the charge which the rulers had made against Jesus to Pilate (v. 12).

The crucifixion detail of four soldiers was permitted to divide the victim's personal items among themselves. All that Jesus had was the clothes that He had been wearing. Now He was naked. A Jew's clothing usually consisted of five items: headdress, shoes, outer garment, girdle, and an inner garment called a *chiton*. Each soldier took one of the first four. But the last was woven without seams. So rather than tear it, they gambled for it. They had no knowledge that they were fulfilling Psalm 22:18. While all of this was going on, the mob about the cross taunted Jesus with jeers and curses. The chief priests themselves joined in with their mockery of Jesus who said that He was the Son of God. If He would come down from the cross, they promised to believe in Him. But the greater miracle of the Resurrection failed to produce such a result.

However, in this scene of utter cruelty there was one tender note. Standing near the cross was Mary, Jesus' mother, along with some other women, and "the disciple . . . whom he loved" (vv. 25, 26). Looking down at His mother Jesus nodded toward John as He said, "Woman, behold thy son!" And to John he said, "Behold thy mother" (vv. 26, 27). Thus the one who was nearest and dearest to Him on earth, Jesus bequeathed to the keeping of the beloved disciple. And from that hour he took her unto his own house. One tradition says that for eleven years she lived with John in Jerusalem and died there. Another says that she later went with him to Ephesus and died there at a ripe old age. But in either case we may be sure that Mary found comfort in John, and he never forgot the trust which Jesus had given to him as the Saviour was dying on a cross.

The crucifixion lasted for six hours, from 9:00 A.M. until about 3:00 P.M. During this time Jesus uttered seven sayings from the cross. John records only three of them. The first, mentioned above, came shortly before 3:00 o'clock. Then Jesus withdrew into that mysterious realm of His redemptive death. Darkness had closed in upon the scene. Matthew and Mark record that sometime during this period Jesus evoked His cry of desolation (27:46; 15:34).

And then John notes that Jesus said, "I thirst" (19:28; cf. Psalms 22:15; 69:21). Thirst was one of the greatest sufferings of the crucifixion. The loss of body fluids through bleeding and perspiration made this almost unbearable. At the beginning of the crucifixion Jesus had refused drugged wine. He would face the ordeal in full consciousness. Now just before He died, He asked for a drink of liquid. While He was suffering He gave no thought to His own needs. Now His throat was parched and His tongue was thick. He was about to utter a cry of completion, and He wanted it to be clear and distinct. So He said, "I thirst." A soldier dipped a sponge in vinegar and pressed it to His lips (v. 29).

Then Jesus said, "It is finished" (v. 30). In the Greek this is one word *(tetelestai)*. It is the form of the verb *(teleō)* meaning a state of permanency. The verb means to bring a thing to its intended end or goal. Literally, "It is finished and stands finished." The crucifixion is finished, and never again will it be required. The redemptive work of Jesus *stands finished.*

The Greek papyri sheds light on this word. A kindred verb of the same family *(teleioo)* was used of the act of completing a deed by dating and signing it. So for all who believe in Him Jesus dated and signed (in His blood) the deed of eternal life. This very word *(teleō)* in the form used by Jesus was used in marking a note as "paid." The promissory note of redemption had been paid. One of the richest meanings for us is seen where a father sent his son on a mission. He was not to return until he had finished the mission, or "until you accomplish this for me." The Father sent the Son on the mission of redemption. Now the Son says, "It is finished," or accomplished.

And having said this Jesus "bowed his head, and gave up the ghost" or spirit (v. 30). He delivered it alongside the Father. Matthew says literally, "He dismissed his spirit" (27:50). In essence He said, "The work is finished. You can go now." He laid down His life of His own accord.

Since it was Friday ("the preparation") the Jews did not want the bodies to remain on the cross over the Sabbath. So they requested Pilate to hasten the death of Jesus and the two thieves. This was to be done by breaking their legs. But finding Jesus already dead, the soldiers did not break His legs. However, one of them did thrust a spear into His side, "and forthwith came there out blood and water" (v. 34). This was a fulfillment of Scripture (cf. Exodus 12:46; Zechariah 12:10). His body was pierced, but not broken.

Of further interest is the medical opinion that blood mingled with water indicated a rupture in the walls of Jesus' heart. So He died of a broken heart.

5. *The Burial of Jesus* (19:38-42). After Jesus' death Joseph of Arimathea and Nicodemus came out boldly on His behalf. They requested that Pilate would permit them to bury the Saviour. So having prepared His body (vv. 39, 40), they placed it in Joseph's new tomb in a nearby garden. It was a tomb "wherein was never a man yet laid" (v. 41).

As with Calvary so with the tomb. Its location is not known. Of interest is the fact that the tomb in the Church of the Holy Sepulchre provides space for only one body. Joseph was a married man. Would he not prepare a tomb for his wife also, and for his children if there were any? Gordon's tomb, adjacent to Gordon's Calvary, has two compartments. One has a place for two bodies. The other is incomplete, as though the tomb may have been used prematurely. Just outside this tomb are the ruins of a Byzantine chapel, showing that in that period this was a sacred site. Did they think that this was the tomb of Jesus? These things certainly are not conclusive. But they are suggestive nevertheless.

6. *The Resurrection of Jesus* (20:1-31). To the Jews any part of a day was regarded as a whole day. Jesus was placed in the tomb before sunset on Friday (one day); He remained in the tomb on Saturday (two days); He came forth from the tomb sometime early on Sunday (three days).

Early the first day of the week Mary Magdalene came to the tomb and found it empty. She thought someone had merely moved the body (v. 2). So she ran to tell Peter and John. They hastened to the tomb. John, being the younger, arrived there first, but did not enter the sepulchre. He merely peeped in. When Peter arrived he rushed in and saw the graveclothes lying in an orderly fashion. But it seems to have made no impression on him. John followed him into the tomb, saw the same evidence, and believed. The orderly arrangement of the linen clothes and napkin told him that this was not the result of a grave robbery. It meant that the Lord was risen.

Mary Magdalene remained at the tomb after the others had left. Hers was a lingering love. And it was to her that Jesus first appeared after His Resurrection (vv. 11-17). And after this blessed experience she rushed to share her joy with the other disciples.

That evening the disciples, save Thomas, were assembled behind closed doors. They still feared what the Jewish rulers might do to them. Suddenly Jesus was in their midst. He greeted them with the customary Jewish greeting. "Peace be unto you" (v. 19). The disciples were overjoyed when Jesus showed them His riven hands and side. It was the risen Lord indeed! With this He gave the first of several commissions to go and evangelize the world. And He gave them a foretaste of Pentecost as He breathed upon them, saying, "Receive ye the Holy Ghost [Spirit]" (v. 22).

When Thomas heard about this appearance, he said, "Except I shall see in His hands the print of the nails, and put my finger into the print of the nails, and thrust my hand into his side, I will not believe" (v. 25). But notice that he only demanded the proof of the bodily Resurrection that the others already had (Luke 24:39, 40).

The next Sunday night the disciples, including Thomas, were assembled in the same place (vv. 26-29). And Jesus appeared to them in the same manner as before. Immediately He challenged Thomas to satisfy the demands upon which he had conditioned his faith in the Resurrection of Jesus. But Thomas did none of these things. The appearance of Jesus was enough. He confessed, "My Lord and my God" (v. 28).

Thomas has been called the "doubter." But was he? The issue of the bodily Resurrection was so important that he simply demanded proof of it. And as the result he made the greatest confession of Jesus' deity which fell from the lips of any disciple. He was the only one who called Him God. Thus "Thomas the heroic" (11:16) became "Thomas the faithful." Jesus said that as blessed as he was in his faith, even more blessed are "they that have not seen, yet have believed" (v. 29).

The structure of John's gospel is built about certain "signs" which prove the deity of Jesus. The greatest of these signs is His Resurrection from the dead (cf. Matthew 12:38-40; 16:1-4). So having reached the climax John says, "And many other signs truly did Jesus in the presence of his disciples, which are not written in this book [but in the synoptics?]: but these are written, that ye might believe [keep on believing] that Jesus is the Christ, the Son of God; and that believing ye might have life through his name" (vv. 30, 31).

These words form a fitting conclusion to this gospel. It may be that John originally intended to close it at this point. But before he sent it forth, he added chapter 21. It continues the same style, and presents the same picture of the risen Christ. Why did John add this additional chapter? It may have been to clarify the picture concerning Simon Peter. He had left him in a bad light (18:27: 20:6). But after the Resurrection Jesus had appeared to Peter (Luke 24:34). Furthermore, He had shown that He had forgiven him and restored him to service. The synoptic gospels were written during Peter's lifetime. By the time that John wrote, Peter was dead. So probably as a tribute to him John added the story to his record. How poverty stricken we would be without it!

7. *The Appearance of Jesus in Galilee* (21:1-23). Some of the disciples had returned to Galilee in anticipation of Jesus' promised appearance there on a designated mountain (Matthew 28:16). While they were waiting they went fishing (21:2, 3). After a fruitless or fishless night, from the shore a man told them to cast their nets on the right side of the boat. And they caught a multitude of fishes (vv. 4-6). John recognized this man as Jesus, and told Peter. Peter swam ahead of the boat and came ashore to Jesus. The Lord had a fire going, and had prepared fish and bread for breakfast.

After they had eaten Jesus three times asked Peter if he loved Him. Each time Peter replied that he did. And with each answer Jesus told him to feed His lambs (or sheep) (vv. 15-17). The first time Jesus asked, "Simon, son of Jonas, lovest thou me more than these?" "These" could refer to the boat, nets, and fish. But more likely it refers to the other disciples. Peter had claimed a greater love and loyalty than the others (Mark 14:29; Luke 22:33). In the light of his denials did he still make such a claim?

After the third question of Jesus, "Peter was grieved because he said the third time, Lovest thou me?" (21:17) Why was he grieved? Some see it as the result of Jesus' three questions about love corresponding to the three denials. On the surface that might appear to be so, according to the English version. But the Greek text throws additional light on the matter.

In the first two questions Jesus used the verb for the higher love *(agapaō)*, a divine love which implies absolute loyalty. And Peter answered with a verb denoting a lower love, the love of friendship *(phileō)*. But in the third question Jesus used the lower word. "Do you love me as a friend?" When twice Peter failed to rise to Jesus' standard of love, then Jesus came down to the love of which Peter was capable. It was Peter's failure in this regard which grieved him when Jesus asked "the third time, Lovest thou me?"

Then Jesus reminded Peter that he would one day prove his love of absolute loyalty (v. 18). John notes that Jesus spoke of the way that Peter would die. He had indeed followed Jesus to the end. Tradition says that he was crucified head downward. Jesus had been crucified upright. And since he had denied Him, Peter said that he was not worthy to die as his Lord had died. Whether this be a true story or not, it is a beautiful one.

But Peter was still Peter. His curiosity got the better of him. So he asked Jesus what would happen to John (vv. 20, 21). And Jesus rebuked His problem disciple by telling him that this was none of his business. "If I will that he tarry till I come, what is that to thee?" (v. 23).

8. *An Endorsement and a Claim* (21:24, 25). Verse 24 is written in the first person plural, "We know that his testimony is true." This statement follows the form found in the papyri where one signs an affadavit. It may well be an affadavit by a group of disciples, perhaps Ephesian elders, that this gospel was written by John, and that his testimony about Jesus is true. "Know" expresses a knowledge of deep perception *(oidamen)*.

And then the final verse reverts back to the first person singular, "I suppose . . ." It is John's final word as to the abundance of Jesus' works. If they were all written down, "I suppose that even the world could not contain the books that should be written."

This was John's superlative tribute to Jesus Christ, the Son of God.

FOR FURTHER STUDY

1. Jesus told the disciples to sell their coats, if necessary, in order to buy a sword (Luke 22:36-38). Then He told Peter not to use it (Matthew 26:51-54; John 18:10, 11). Why these different instructions? Read J. B. Phillips and Revised Version of Luke 22:36-38.

2. For a full account of the trial of Jesus read Robertson's *A Harmony of the Gospels,* pp. 209-225.

3. Read the article "Pilate" in Hastings *Dictionary of the Bible*, pp. 729, 730, and in *The Zondervan Pictorial Bible Dictionary*.
4. Read the article "Crucifixion" in Hastings, *op. cit.*, p. 170, and *The Zondervan Pictorial Bible Dictionary*.
5. Compare Psalm 22 with the account of the crucifixion of Jesus in the four gospels, noting the prophetic nature of this psalm.
6. Is there a positive relationship between honest doubt and true faith? What benefits of faith may we derive from Thomas' doubt? In what way may we be more blessed than Thomas in our faith?
7. For the significance of John 21:24 read Hobbs, *Preaching Values From the Papyri* (Baker), pp. 84-88.